PARTY COSTUMES
for kids

PARTY COSTUMES
for kids

Jean Greenhowe

A DAVID & CHARLES CRAFT BOOK

British Library Cataloguing in Publication Data

Greenhowe, Jean
  Party costumes for kids.
  1. children's fancy dress. Making – Manuals
  I. Title
  646.4'7

ISBN 0–7153–9230–1

Text & diagrams © Jean Greenhowe 1988

Diagrams by Eadan Art

Border stencils by Wren Loasby

Photographs © *Woman's Weekly*, IPC Magazines 1988

Typeset by ABM Typographics Ltd, Hull
and printed in The Netherlands
by Royal Smeets Offset Weert
for David & Charles Publishers plc
Brunel House Newton Abbot Devon

Distributed in the United States by
Sterling Publishing Co, Inc,
2, Park Avenue, New York, NY 10016

Contents

Introduction

Dressing up in mum's or dad's old clothes is one of the many pleasures of childhood, but there are times when a special costume is required and this can be quite a problem for those who are not expert dressmakers.

The outfits in this book have been designed with this in mind. Best of all, they can be made to fit any size of child, since the instructions are written so as to encompass all size variations at each stage of making and a perfect fit is guaranteed.

About half the costumes are constructed from simple shapes, such as rectangles and circles, and sometimes everyday items of clothing are used as a basis and only a few extra oddments need to be made. Any necessary patterns are kept as straightforward as possible, with the shapes printed onto grids, which can be drawn onto dressmaker's graph paper.

Once you know how to construct a bodice from straight strips of fabric, or how to put together a pair of pants, then the possibilities are endless. Let your imagination run riot, be as extravagant with fabrics and trimmings as you wish – the results are sure to be enchanting and much admired!

General Techniques

Children's sizes and material quantities

When designing a costume, I have to make it in a specific size, so that it can be photographed on a model. The size chosen is always for height 100-110cm (3ft 3in-3ft 7in) or age 3-5 years. However, all the costumes can be made to fit any size. Although it is difficult to be precise about an upper height or age limit (since some of the outfits could easily be adapted to suit teenagers or adults), in general, they are most suitable for children up to 12 years or 150cm (4ft 11in) in height.

The quantities of materials quoted are for heights up to 110cm (3ft 7in), but in *every case* where more fabric will be needed for taller children, there are notes to indicate exactly how much extra is required for all larger sizes.

Metric and imperial measurements

All the measurements throughout the book have been worked out individually both in metric and imperial sizes, so that they are not always accurate conversions from one set to the other. This has been done to avoid having awkward measurements, when a little extra either way will make no difference to the garment.

In the same way, the material quantities are to the nearest required for each garment, and conversions are not always exactly the same for other garments. Use either metric or imperial throughout as preferred.

Equipment

You will need only the usual items required for household sewing – a sewing-machine, assorted sewing threads, sewing needles, large and small scissors, tape measure and ruler.

Pins should be the large glass-headed variety, since these are much easier to handle and see than the ordinary dressmaking kind.

A yardstick or a long straight piece of wood will be found very useful for drawing straight lines onto fabric. You will also need a pair of inexpensive school-type compasses for drawing small circles.

Glue

When adhesive is quoted in the instructions, it should be a quick-drying type such as UHU all-purpose adhesive, unless otherwise specified.

Drawing the patterns

You will need dressmaker's graph paper, either metric or imperial. All the patterns are drawn onto grids, where each square on every grid equals 5cm (2in). Copy the pattern outlines onto the graph paper, drawing the shape of the pattern one square at a time. Cut out and use the paper pattern as directed.

Drawing large circles

Where large circular, or quarter circle, patterns are required, these can be drawn as follows.

You will need a piece of paper of sufficient size (for example, brown wrapping-paper), a drawing-pin, a pencil and a length of string. For a full circular pattern, the paper will have to be folded into quarters before drawing.

Tie a knot in one end of the string so that

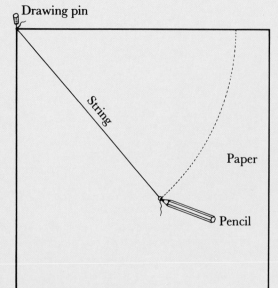

DIAGRAM 1 *drawing a large circular or quarter-circle pattern*

the pencil point can be pushed through it. Measure the length required along the string from the knot. Tie a knot here and push the drawing-pin through it. This measurement will be the radius of the circle, which is half the diameter (the distance across the circle). Now draw the quarter circle as shown in Diagram 1. The diagram shows a quarter circle drawn on a single sheet of paper, but the procedure is exactly the same for paper which has been folded into quarters. Cut out the pattern along the drawn line.

Fabrics
Cast-off items of clothing, bed-sheets and curtains can often be picked up in thrift or charity shops to provide useful and inexpensive fabric for making children's costumes. In particular, any garment made from lurex fabric will probably work out cheaper than buying equivalent fabric by the metre or yard.

Fabrics are now available in many different widths, but for convenience, the most often quoted width in the instructions is 91cm (36in). It does not matter if the fabric you choose is wider than this.

Non-woven curtain fabric is used for some of the garments and you can see it quite clearly in the Robin Hood costume (p22). This fabric is rather like felt, since it does not fray at the cut edges and so requires little finishing.

Cutting out
Guidance is given throughout the instructions for placing the pattern pieces on the fabric when cutting out. For any pattern edges which have to be placed to a fold, this means that the piece will be cut from double fabric, with the folded edge of the fabric level with this edge of the pattern.

Seams
All seams and turnings throughout the book are 1cm (⅜in), unless otherwise stated. Hems on garments are usually 2cm (¾in), the raw edge being turned in 1cm (⅜in) when the hem is stitched in place.

Join all pieces with right sides of fabric together and press all seams open, unless other instructions are given.

The raw edges of the seams do not need to be finished unless you are using fabric which frays badly. In this case, either machine stitch or overlock the raw edges, or oversew by hand. Finishing the seams will, of course, make the garment more durable.

Gathering
Loosen the top tension on your sewing-machine and set to a fairly long stitch length. Make a row of machine stitches on the fabric at the seam line, 1cm (⅜in) away from the raw edge. Now pull the bobbin thread at each end of the stitching line while you push the fabric along, to gather to the required measurement. Knot the ends of threads to prevent the gathers from slipping. Space out the gathers evenly before sewing them in place.

To stitch on a waistband
This is described as 'binding' in the instructions and it is exactly like sewing on bias binding. First, stitch one long edge of the waistband to the gathered edge of the garment, having the right sides together, the raw edges level and letting the ends of the waistband extend either 1cm (⅜in) (or the required amount for an overlap), beyond the ends of the garment. Turn in the remaining long raw edge 1cm (⅜in) and stitch the folded edge in place over the first seam line, thus enclosing the raw edges of the fabric (see Diagram 2). Turn in the raw edges at the ends of the waistband and stitch also.

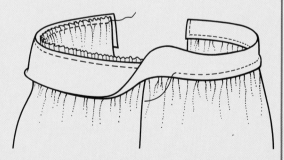

DIAGRAM 2 *how to sew on a waist band*

Garment fastenings
You can use buttons, hooks and eyes, snap-fasteners or strips of Velcro.

When a dress is composed of a skirt and

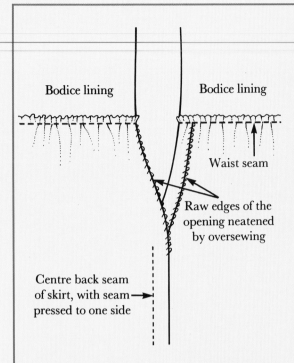

DIAGRAM 3 *the back opening on a dress skirt and bodice, showing the overlap*

bodice, there will be an opening on the back skirt seam. This seam is pressed to one side to provide an overlap of fabric to correspond with the overlap on the back edges of the bodice (see Diagram 3).

For a skirt or pair of trousers which has a waistband, the back seam is pressed to one side also to provide an overlap in the same way.

Velcro fastener
This is sold by the centimetre or inch and is available from fabric shops and haberdashery departments in a variety of colours.

Velcro is composed of two flat narrow nylon strips: one strip has hundreds of tiny hooks and the other has a furry surface composed of minute loops. When the strips are pressed firmly together, the hooks catch in the loops and the strips cannot be pulled apart sideways. However, they can be separated by peeling them apart.

Velcro is very useful to fasten children's garments because it allows for a certain amount of adjustment in fit when fastening, which would not be possible on other fixed fastenings such as buttons or snap-fasteners.

Threading elastic through casings
Fasten a safety-pin into one end of the elastic and thread it through the fabric casings.

Sometimes a seam will be in the way of the safety-pin, making it difficult to push through. For example, the elasticated waist of a pair of pants will have two seams in the way. To avoid this problem, trim the seams before stitching the casing as shown in Diagram 4.

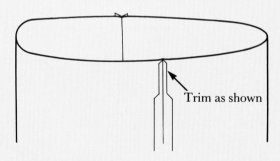

DIAGRAM 4 *trimming seams before stitching a casing for the elastic*

Polynesian Girl

The sarong and bra-top can be stitched up in minutes and although the lei (the flower garland) looks as though it might be complicated, it is quite easy to make. The flowers are fashioned from strips of crêpe paper and when they are threaded, each one falls into place to form a rounded garland of colourful blooms.

SARONG AND BRA-TOP
You will need
1m (1⅛yd) of 91cm (36in) wide soft cotton fabric printed with large flowers
90cm (1yd) of soft cord, such as cotton piping-cord

To make the bra-top
Cut a 22cm (9in) wide strip right across one end of the 91cm (36in) width of the fabric. Fold the strip, bringing the short ends together. Now trim the long edges, tapering to a rounded point at centre of short ends as shown in Diagram 1. Hem all round the edge.

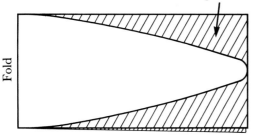

Trim off the shaded portions

Fold

DIAGRAM 1 *tapering the fabric strip*

Fold the length of cord in half and pass the looped end around the centre of fabric strip. Push the ends of the cord through the loop and pull ends tightly to gather up the fabric.

Place the bra-top around the child and knot the tapered ends at the back. Tie the cord in a bow at back of neck.

To make the sarong
Take the remaining piece of fabric and wrap one of the 91cm (36in) edges around the child's waist, then knot the corners at one side as shown in the illustration. Check the length of the sarong, which should be about the same as shown in the illustration. Mark the fabric and trim off any excess length if necessary. Hem all the raw edges.

LEI
You will need
60cm (⅝yd) of soft cord such as cotton piping-cord
One packet of green crêpe paper
Two packets of different colours of crêpe paper to tone with flowers on the bra and sarong
Strong sewing thread
A hair-grip
Adhesive

To cut the crêpe paper
For the flower petals, keep one of the packets of coloured crêpe paper folded as purchased, then cut a 3.5cm (1⅜in) section off one end as shown in Diagram 2. When making the flowers, continue cutting off sections as required. Unfold the paper strip and cut it into 40cm (16in) lengths. Each 40cm (16in) length will make one flower. Gently stretch the crêpe paper at one long edge of each flower. Cut and make flowers from remaining packet of coloured crêpe paper in the same way.

For the stamens, cut a 3.5cm (1⅜in) section off the packet of green crêpe paper in the same way as for the flowers. When making the flowers, continue cutting off sections for the stamens as required. Keeping the section folded, snip one long edge into fine points, leaving the opposite edge uncut as shown in Diagram 3. Unfold the paper strip and cut into lengths of three or four points for each flower.

For the leaves, cut a 5cm (2in) section off the green crêpe paper, keeping the paper folded as before. When making the flowers, continue cutting off sections for the leaves as required. Cut one long edge of the section into pointed leaf shapes leaving the opposite edge uncut as shown in Diagram 4. Unfold the paper strip and cut it into lengths of four or five leaves for each flower.

To make one flower
Glue the straight edge of the stamens to one end of the flower strip at the unstretched edge. Roll up the flower strip, pleating and gathering the unstretched edge as you go.

Wind the uncut edge of one of the leaf strips around the base of the flower. Use a length of sewing thread to bind around the base and knot ends together.

To thread the flowers
Cut the piece of cord into equal lengths and make a knot at one end of each one. Thread a darning needle with a 2m (2¼yd) length of strong thread and knot ends of thread together. Sew to knotted end of one cord. Thread flowers onto the double thread, pushing the needle through the narrow base of each flower as shown in Diagram 5.

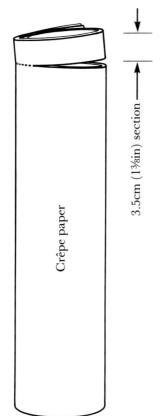

DIAGRAM 2 *cutting a section off the crêpe paper*

3.5cm (1⅜in) section

Crêpe paper

DIAGRAM 3 *snipping the crêpe paper to form stamens*

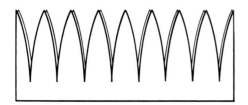

DIAGRAM 4 *cutting the crêpe paper into leaf shapes*

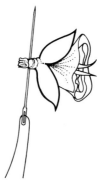

DIAGRAM 5 *threading on the flowers*

Continue making and threading on flowers, alternating the colours as desired, until you have a 70cm (28in) long garland. Sew on the knotted end of remaining cord. Use the lengths of cord to tie lei at back of neck, adjusting length to suit the child.

Flowers in hair
Make a few more crêpe-paper flowers and sew them to the hair-grip.

Captain Crimson

This swashbuckling hero wears a jacket made fom a second-hand curtain!
The splendid full-sleeved 'shirt' could not be easier to make. An ordinary shirt is worn under
the jacket and the full sleeves are straight strips of fabric sewn into the jacket armholes.

BASIS FOR COSTUME
Ordinary white shirt
Track-suit pants or leggings, close-fitting
Black wellington boots
A wide-brimmed cavalier-type hat from a
    toyshop, or see p90 to make the hat
A few large feathers or lengths of marabou
    feather trimming for decorating the hat
Toy sword, with hilt as illustration
A long scarf for the waist sash, or see below

BOOT TOPS
20cm (¼yd) of 91cm (36in) wide, black
    leather cloth or felt
Double-sided sticky tape or adhesive
Metric or imperial graph paper

To make
Copy the boot-top pattern outline onto graph
paper square by square. Place the top edge of
the pattern around the top edge of one boot to
see if it fits, allowing for 5mm (¼in) extra on
each centre-back edge for the seam. Lengthen
or shorten the back edges of pattern if necessary.

Cut two boot-top pieces from leather cloth
or felt and join the centre-back edges with a
5mm (¼in) seam. Glue the seams open.

Put the boot tops on the boots, right side
out, having seams at centre back, and top
edges extending 1cm (⅜in) above tops of
boots. If you wish to fix the boot tops in place
temporarily, place strips of double-sided tape
all round the inside of top edges of the boots.

Turn top edges to inside of boots and fix
them to sticky tape or glue in place.

JACKET
90cm (1yd) of 91cm (36in) wide, non-woven
    curtain fabric or felt*
3.50m (3⅞yd) of 1cm (⅜in) wide braid
2.40m (2¾yd) of 2cm (¾in) wide braid

7 large fancy buttons
Metric or imperial graph paper

*Note: The finished back length of the jacket is
55cm (22in) from back neck to hem. The jacket
should be about mid-thigh length. Try the
pattern against the child and adjust length as
necessary. If the pattern needs to be
lengthened a lot, then add twice the extra
length required to the amount of fabric quoted.

From Diagram 2, you will see that it is possible to cut the jacket pieces a bit longer than the
pattern, so extra fabric may not be necessary.

The finished jacket also measures 70cm
(27¾in) around the chest and it should be
loose enough for the edges to meet easily at
centre front. If the jacket pattern needs to be
widened considerably, then you will simply
need to buy fabric which is wider than 91cm
(36in). See Diagram 1 showing how to
lengthen and widen the pattern.

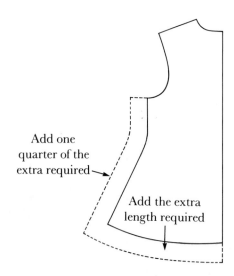

Add one
quarter of the
extra required →

Add the extra
length required
↓

DIAGRAM 1 *how to lengthen and widen the*
pattern for larger sizes

To make

Copy the pattern outlines onto graph paper square by square. Referring to Diagram 2, cut out the jacket and shoulder pieces as shown. Turn in centre front edges of the jacket front pieces 1cm (³⁄8in) and stitch down. For the mock button-holes, cut fourteen 12cm (4³⁄4in) lengths of the narrow braid. Fold each length having the cut ends side by side and flattening at the folded end to mitre as shown on the jacket pattern. Stitch seven lengths to each front edge as shown on the pattern, spacing them 6cm (2¹⁄4in) apart. The raw ends will be covered by the wide braid later on.

Now join jacket fronts to back at the shoulder and side edges. Clip seams at waist curves. Clip the armhole and neck edges at curves, within the seam allowance. Turn in these edges 1cm (³⁄8in) and stitch down. Turn in hem edge in the same way and stitch down. Sew the wide braid down the centre front and the hem edges, mitring at the corners. Sew narrow braid around the neck edge, easing it around the curves.

Join the shoulder pieces in pairs along the curved edges only. Trim seams, turn right side out and press. Stitch the straight edges of each piece together. Sew narrow braid around the curved edges, easing braid to fit the curves.

Now pin the straight edges 1cm (³⁄8in) inside armholes of jacket, matching the centre points to shoulder seams of jacket. Stitch in place as pinned. Sew narrow braid all around each armhole edge of the jacket, easing braid around the curves.

Sew buttons to the mock buttonholes on right front edge of the jacket.

SLEEVES

40cm (¹⁄2yd) of 91cm (36in) wide, heavy
 cotton fabric*
90cm (1yd) of 6cm (2¹⁄4in) wide, white lace
 edging
40cm (¹⁄2yd) of narrow elastic

*Note: The 40cm (¹⁄2yd) measurement is the sleeve length from the jacket shoulder seam to the wrist and it should be generous enough to blouse at the wrist when worn. If longer sleeves are required, buy more fabric accordingly.

To make

Fold the fabric, bringing the selvedges together, then cut along the fold. Hem one 45.5cm (18in) edge of each sleeve to form casings for the elastic. Stitch lace to each folded hemmed edge. Thread elastic through casings to fit the child's wrists. Secure elastic at each end of the casings. Join the 40cm (¹⁄2yd) edges of each sleeve and lace edging, for underarm seams.

Neaten the remaining raw edges with narrow hems or overlocking on the machine. Having right sides of sleeves and jacket outside, pin these neatened edges of sleeves 1cm (³⁄8in) inside armhole edges of the jacket, easing in fullness. Slip stitch in place as pinned.

SASH

Two 25 x 80cm (10 x 32in) strips of fabric
50cm (⁵⁄8yd) of silver- or gold-fringed trimming

To make

Join the fabric strips at one pair of short edges, then hem all the remaining raw edges. Sew the fringed trimming to the ends. Tie sash with loop as shown in photo.

DIAGRAM 2 *cutting the jacket pieces*

Folded width of the fabric

JACKET BACK

Folded edge

Selvedges

90cm (1yd) length of fabric

JACKET FRONTS

SHOULDER PIECE

SHOULDER PIECE

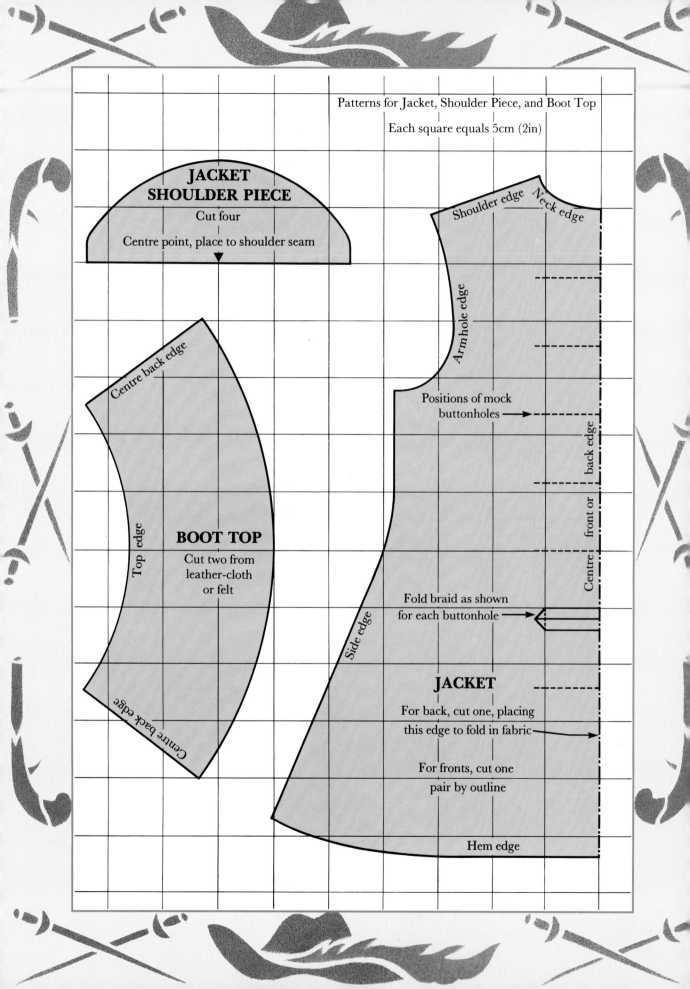

**JACKET
SHOULDER PIECE**

Cut four

Centre point, place to shoulder seam

Patterns for Jacket, Shoulder Piece, and Boot Top

Each square equals 5cm (2in)

Shoulder edge

Neck edge

Armhole edge

Centre back edge

Positions of mock
buttonholes →

Centre front or back edge

BOOT TOP

Cut two from
leather-cloth
or felt

Top edge

Side edge

Fold braid as shown
for each buttonhole →

JACKET

For back, cut one, placing
this edge to fold in fabric →

For fronts, cut one
pair by outline

Centre back edge

Hem edge

Ballerina

This romantic, fairy-tale dress is made mostly from net, using vivid pink over layers of white, with glittery pink lamé fabric for the bodice, shoulder straps and rosettes. Satin dress fabric, or shiny dress-lining material, could be used as an inexpensive alternative to the lamé.

BASIS FOR COSTUME
Ballet dancing pumps
A posy of artificial or fresh flowers

DRESS AND HEAD-DRESS
You will need
2m (2¼yd) of 138cm (54in) wide coloured net fabric*
4m (4½yd) of 138cm (54in) wide white net fabric*
80cm (⅞yd) of 91cm (36in) wide lamé fabric to tone with the coloured net
Transparent nylon sewing thread
Fastenings for dress bodice
A short length of narrow elastic for head-dress

*Note: Instructions are for a finished skirt length of 49cm (19½in). The skirt can be made up to 69cm (27in) in length if necessary, but a little more fabric will be needed in order to complete the net frills at hem, neckline and for the head-dress. An extra 25cm (¼yd) of coloured net and 50cm (½yd) of white net will be ample to meet these requirements.

To make the bodice
Cut two strips of lamé fabric (one for the bodice and one for the lining) to the measurements given in Diagram 1. As a general guide, for a child of 100-110cm (3ft 3in-3ft 7in) in height, the *width* of each strip should be about 16cm (6¼in), which includes seam allowances. Join the pieces all round the edges, leaving a gap in one long edge for turning. Trim the corners of the seam. Turn right side out and press, then slip stitch the gap.

For the shoulder straps, cut two 8 x 34cm (3 x 13½in) strips of lamé fabric. Join the long edges and across one short end of each strip. Trim seams and corners. Turn straps right side out and press.

Put the bodice around the child, then overlap and pin short edges at centre back as necessary, to fit the chest neatly. Pin the ends of the shoulder straps to the bodice at the front and the back, adjusting length of straps as necessary, so that top edge of bodice fits just under the arms as shown in Diagram 2. Now pin a small dart at each side of the bodice (through all layers of fabric), to fit the bodice neatly to the child's waist as shown in Diagram 2.

Remove the bodice and adjust strap positions if necessary, so that they are exactly the same distance apart and equal in length. Stitch along the top edge of the bodice and through the straps. Trim any excessive length off the

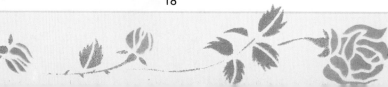

Cut length of each strip, the child's chest measurement
plus 6cm (2¼in) for seams and overlap

Cut width of each strip, the child's underarm to waist measurement plus 2cm (¾in) for seam allowances

DIAGRAM 1 *measurements for the bodice fabric strips*

18

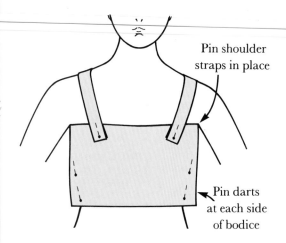

Pin shoulder
straps in place

Pin darts
at each side
of bodice

DIAGRAM 2 *fitting the bodice on the child*

straps, then sew the ends in place. Stitch the darts as pinned, through all thicknesses of fabric. Note that darts and ends of straps will be on the inside (wrong side) of the bodice when making up the rest of the dress.

To make the skirt
The net fabric will be folded in half across the width when purchased. Keep it folded when you cut out the skirt pieces. If extra fabric has been purchased for the frills, cut this off the nets before you start on the skirt, and lay aside.

You will now have one 2m (2¼yd) length of coloured net and one 4m (4½yd) length of white net. Cut the white net into two 2m (2¼yd) lengths. Pin the three equal lengths of net together all along the folded edges as shown in Diagram 3.

Measure 44cm (17½in), or the required skirt length, from the folded edges by inserting pins through the nets at regular intervals as shown in Diagram 3. Cut the net to skirt length, leaving the pins in the remaining

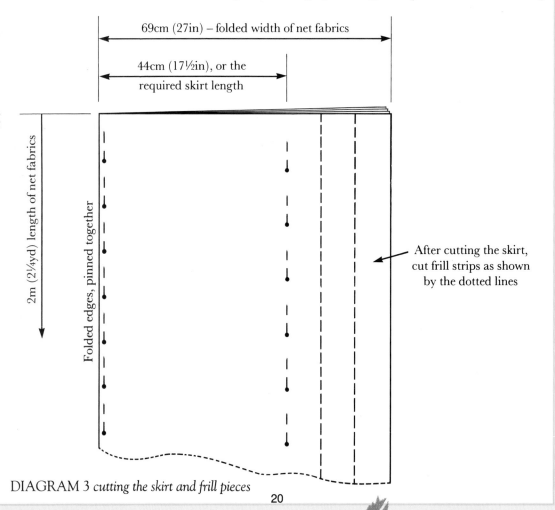

69cm (27in) – folded width of net fabrics

44cm (17½in), or the
required skirt length

2m (2¼yd) length of net fabrics

Folded edges, pinned together

After cutting the skirt,
cut frill strips as shown
by the dotted lines

DIAGRAM 3 *cutting the skirt and frill pieces*

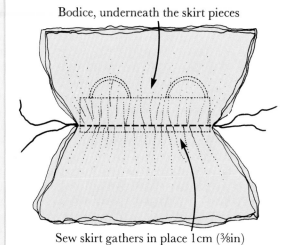

Bodice, underneath the skirt pieces

Sew skirt gathers in place 1cm (⅜in)
up from waist edge of bodice

DIAGRAM 4 *sewing the skirt to the bodice*

pieces of net so that they are held together as
you cut the skirt. Cut the frill strips 8cm (3in)
wide from the remaining pieces of net, using
pins to measure as for the skirt. Note that if
extra fabric was purchased and laid aside for
the frills, the frill strips should be cut across the
width of these fabric pieces.

Unfold all the three *skirt* net pieces and
place the coloured net underneath the two
white pieces. Gather the skirt pieces along the
centre fold line through all the net layers. Pull
up the gathers to fit the waist edge of bodice.
Keeping the skirt pieces opened up as when
gathering, pin, then sew, the gathers to the
right side of the bodice 1cm (⅜in) up from the
waist edge, as shown in Diagram 4. Take care
when you do this to have the coloured net
against the bodice and the white net uppermost. Now fold the skirt down, away from the
bodice.

The short edges of each separate skirt strip
now have to be joined, using transparent sewing thread. Lap the short edges of each one
1cm (⅜in) and stitch from the hem edge upwards, leaving 16cm (6½in) open at the other
end of each seam for back waist opening. Sew
fastenings to back edges of the bodice.

To make the frills
The frills are composed of three strips of net,
two layers of white and one coloured layer on

top of the white layers. The gathers should be
made about 3cm (1¼in) away from one set of
long edges.

For a quick and easy method of gathering,
place one end of the three frill strips together
under the machine foot, then, as you stitch,
push the fabric in small tucks under the
machine foot. When you are near the end of
one length, feed in another, overlapping the
ends of the first and second. Gather up strips of
net as described, to make a 4m (4½yd) continuous length.

When sewing the frills in place, stitch
through the gathers. Sew a frill to the outer net
layer of the skirt, around the lower edge.

For the bodice frill, cut a 1m (1yd) length of
frill. Pin the centre of the length to the centre-
front top edge of the bodice. Continue pinning
the frill in place as far as the shoulder straps.
Leave a 20cm (8in) length of frill at each side
unattached (to pass around the arms), then pin
the frill to the top back edges of bodice between shoulder straps and back edges. Trim off
excess length of frill, then stitch in place as
pinned.

To make the rosettes
Draw, then cut out, a 10cm (4in) diameter circle of paper. Use this as a pattern to cut out
twenty-four circles from the lamé fabric. Note
that several circles can be cut at one time by
pinning the pattern to a few layers of fabric.

Turn in the raw edge of each circle 5mm
(¼in) and run round a gathering thread. Pull
up the gathers tightly and fasten off. Flatten
the rosette, having the gathers at the centre,
then sew through gathers to centre of circle
and back again. Fasten off.

Sew four rosettes to the bodice, one at the
end of each shoulder strap as shown in the
illustration. Sew the remaining rosettes at
regular intervals around the hem frill.

To make the head-dress
The head-dress can be worn around a top-knot
of hair as shown in the illustration, or around
the child's head. Cut a length of frill, making it
a little shorter than required. Sew a short
length of elastic to the ends. Make two rosettes
as described and sew them to the centre front
of the head-dress.

Robin Hood

This outfit is made from non-woven curtain fabric, which does not fray, but felt would make a good substitute. A permanent black marker-pen is used for the 'stitching' lines.

BASIS FOR COSTUME

Green tights

A green or brown sweater

A pair of man's socks for the boots, to be worn over everyday shoes

A sword and bow and arrow, from a toyshop

TUNIC, HOOD, CAP AND BELT

You will need

70cm (¾yd) of 122cm (48in) wide green non-woven fabric or felt*

90cm (1yd) of 122cm (48in) wide tan non-woven fabric or felt

50cm (½yd) of cord for hood fastening

Black permanent marker-pen

A strip of leather cloth or felt, and a buckle, for the belt

A few feathers for cap

Metric or imperial graph paper

*Note: When made up, the tunic measures 84cm (33in) around the chest, which should be generous enough to fit most sizes. If the tunic needs to be made larger, add the extra to side edges of tunic pattern.

The tunic measures 45cm (18in) from back neck to lower edge when finished. If you wish to lengthen it, add the extra to lower edge of pattern, then add this amount to the green fabric requirements. The tunic should be upper-thigh length on the child.

To make the tunic

Copy the pattern outline onto graph paper square by square and all the dotted neck lines also.

See Diagram 1 for the method of folding the green fabric when cutting out. Cut the back piece first. Trim the pattern on the front neck edge cutting line and keep this piece of pattern for later. Cut the front tunic piece.

Join tunic front to back at the shoulder edges. Turn in the sleeve edges 1cm (⅜in) and stitch down. Cut two 6 x 32cm (2¼ x 12¾in) strips of tan fabric for the sleeve trimming. Turn in long edges of the strips 1cm (⅜in) and stitch down. Using the marker pen and a ruler, mark stitching lines 1cm (⅜in) away from long edges of each strip on the right side. Place the strips right side up, over the right side of sleeve edges of the tunic, letting one long edge of each strip extend slightly beyond sleeve edge of the tunic. Stitch the strips in place.

Clip the curves in back neck edge of tunic within the seam allowance. Clip at centre front V-point also. Turn in the neck edges 1cm (⅜in) and stitch down.

Now rejoin the piece of tunic pattern to the main pattern with sticky tape. Trace off patterns for the neck edge strips, one for front and one for back, at the dotted lines shown. Cut one of each piece, placing patterns to folds in the tan fabric.

Join the front neck piece to back piece at the shoulder edges. Turn in all the raw edges, clipping curve and V-point, then stitch down. Mark stitching lines with pen as before. Stitch the neck piece to tunic in same way as for the sleeve strips.

Join tunic front to back at the side edges. Clip seams at the underarm curves. Trim seams at the position of the sleeve edging strips.

Turn in the lower edge of tunic 1cm (⅜in) and stitch down. Cut two 6 x 44cm (2¼ x 17½in) strips of tan fabric, noting that if you have widened the tunic, the lengths will have to be adjusted to fit. Join strips to each other at the short edges. Hem the long edges and mark stitching lines as for the sleeve strips. Stitch to lower edge of tunic in same way as for the sleeve strips.

To make the hood

For the collar, cut a 48cm (19in) diameter circle of tan fabric. Cut a 10cm (4in) diameter circle from the centre for the neck edge and discard this small circle. Now cut away one quarter of the circle and discard this piece. Turn in the edges of collar 1cm (3/8in) except for the neck edge, and stitch down. Clip the neck edge curve within the seam allowance. Mark seamed edges of the collar with stitching lines, using pen as before.

For the hood, cut a 25 x 64cm (10 x 25¼in) strip of tan fabric. Bring the short edges of the strip together, then join the long edges at one side. Turn in the remaining long edge 1cm (3/8in) and stitch down. Mark this edge with stitching lines.

Gather the remaining raw edge of the hood to fit the neck edge of the collar, then stitch in place, with right sides of both together and raw edges level. Trim the seam, then stitch on a strip of the tan fabric to neaten and cover raw edges of seam, enclosing the end of a 25cm (¼yd) length of cord at each end of neck for the ties.

To make the cap

Draw the cap pattern onto graph paper. The finished cap will measure 54cm (21¼in) around the lower tan strip. This size can be adjusted by cutting the pattern vertically from lower to upper edge at the widest point. Then either lap these edges to make smaller, or insert an extra strip to make larger.

Cut one pair of cap pieces from green fabric. Join them, leaving the lower edges open. Trim the seam. Turn in lower edge 1cm (3/8in) and stitch down. Cut a 6 x 56cm (2¼ x 22in) strip of tan fabric, or the length required plus seam allowance, if you have adjusted the cap pattern.

Join short edges of the strip, then turn in long edges, stitch and mark with pen as for the other strips. With right sides out, pin the strip over the lower edge of the cap so that hemmed edge of cap runs along the centre of the strip. Stitch in place as pinned along centre of strip only. Sew the feathers to one side of the cap.

To make the belt

Cut the strip of leather cloth or felt to suit the buckle. Attach buckle to one end and make holes at intervals in the other end.

DIAGRAM 1 *cutting the tunic pieces from green fabric*

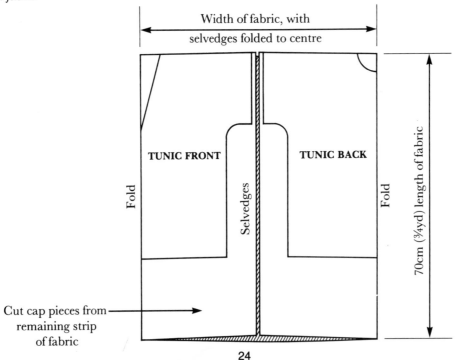

Width of fabric, with selvedges folded to centre

TUNIC FRONT

TUNIC BACK

Fold

Selvedges

Fold

70cm (¾yd) length of fabric

Cut cap pieces from remaining strip of fabric

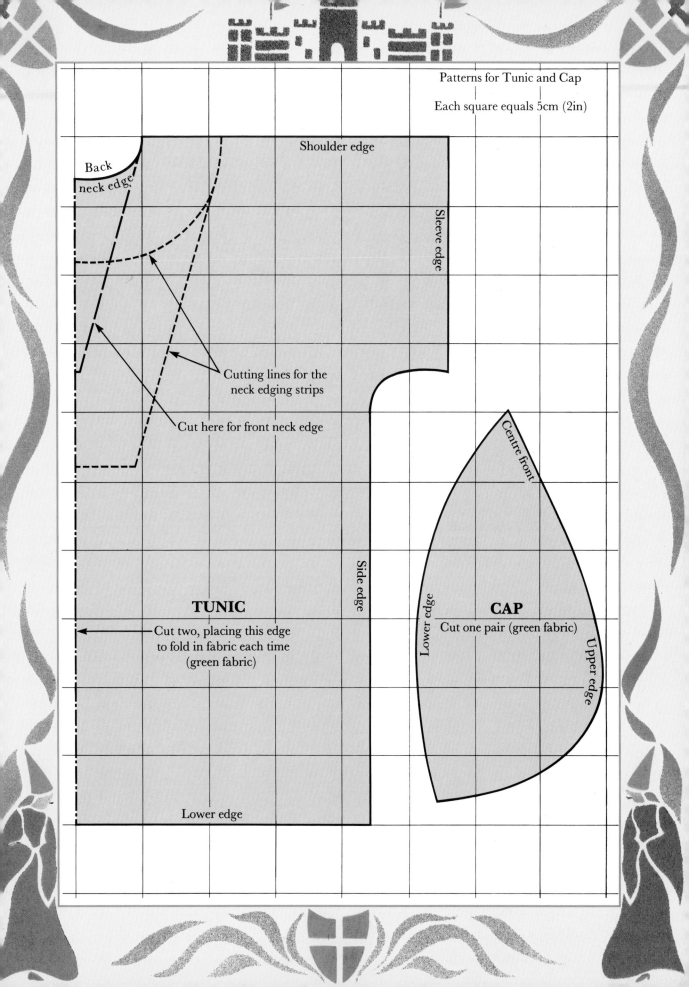

Patterns for Tunic and Cap

Each square equals 5cm (2in)

Shoulder edge

Back neck edge

Sleeve edge

Cutting lines for the neck edging strips

Cut here for front neck edge

Side edge

TUNIC

Cut two, placing this edge to fold in fabric each time (green fabric)

Lower edge

Centre front

Lower edge

CAP

Cut one pair (green fabric)

Upper edge

Hoe-down Gal

*Hoe-down gal, in her demure gingham dress, is all ready for the square dance.
Two different sizes of gingham checks are used and the dress has a full circular skirt
with an attached frilled net underskirt for extra bounce. No special patterns are
required for making, just straight strips and a circle for the skirt.*

BASIS FOR COSTUME
A pair of slipperettes or suitable shoes

DRESS
You will need
1.70m (1⅞yd) of 91cm (36in) wide
  small-check gingham fabric
1.40m (1⅝yd) of 91cm (36in) wide
  large-check gingham fabric*
1.70m (1⅞yd) of 138cm (54in) wide white
  net fabric for the underskirt*
3.50m (3⅞yd) of ric-rac braid in a colour to
  contrast with dress fabric
Oddment of ribbon to match ric-rac braid
40cm (½yd) of narrow elastic
Fastenings for dress bodice and skirt opening

*Note: Instructions are given for a dress skirt
with a possible waist to a hem length of up to
43cm (17in), according to where the frill is attached. If the skirt needs to be shorter than
this, the adjustment can be made when the
skirt is made up. The skirt should be above
knee length on the child. If a skirt longer than
43cm (17in) is required, the extra length
should be added to the skirt frill, so add four
times the extra length needed, to the large-

check gingham and the net fabric requirements.
See cutting layout for the large-check fabric.
The amount quoted for the small-check fabric
is sufficient for all sizes.

Cutting out the pieces
When cutting out all the pieces, refer to the
cutting layouts given for each different fabric.
When cutting the straight strips from gingham, simply follow the straight lines of the
checks, making sure that they will match when
you join them for the frill strips.

To make the bodice
Cut two strips of small-check fabric (one for
the bodice and one for the lining) to the
measurements given in Diagram 1. As a general
guide, for a child of 100-110cm (3ft 3in-3ft
7in) the *width* of each strip should be about
16cm (6¼in), which includes seam allowances. Join the pieces around the edges, leaving one pair of long edges open. Trim corners
of seam, turn right side out and press. Tack the
long raw edges together, for waist edge of
bodice.

For the shoulder straps, cut two 8 x 34cm (3
x 13½in) strips of small-check fabric. Join the
long edges and across one short end of each

Cut length of each strip, the child's chest measurement
plus 6cm (2¼in) for seams and overlap

Cut width of each strip,
the child's underarm to
waist measurement plus
2cm (¾in) for seam
allowances

DIAGRAM 1 *measurements for the bodice fabric strips*

strip. Trim seams and corners. Turn straps right side out and press.

Put the bodice around the child, then overlap and pin short edges at centre back as necessary, to fit the chest neatly. Pin the ends of the shoulder straps to the bodice at the front and back, adjusting length of straps as necessary, so that the top edge of bodice fits just under the arms as shown in Diagram 2. Now pin a small dart at each side of the bodice (through all layers of fabric), to fit the bodice neatly to the child's waist as shown in Diagram 2.

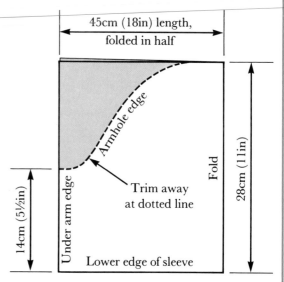

DIAGRAM 3 *cutting the sleeve strips to shape*

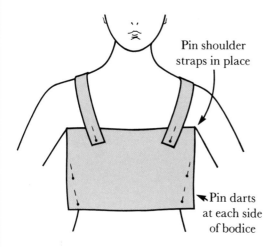

DIAGRAM 2 *fitting the bodice on the child*

Remove the bodice and adjust strap positions if necessary, so that they are exactly the same distance apart and equal in length. Stitch along the top edge of the bodice and through the straps. Trim any excessive length off the straps, then sew the ends in place. Stitch darts as pinned, through all thicknesses of fabric. Note that darts and ends of straps will be on the inside (wrong side) of the bodice when you make up the rest of the dress.

To make the sleeves

Cut two 28 x 45cm (11 x 18in) strips of small-check fabric. Fold each sleeve strip and trim to shape as shown in Diagram 3. Join the short underarm edges of each sleeve. Turn in lower edge of each sleeve 5mm (¼in), then 6cm (2¼in) and press. Stitch the folded-in edges in place, leaving gaps in stitching for inserting the elastic. Stitch again 1cm (⅜in) away from first stitching line through the double thick-

ness of fabric to complete the casing for the elastic.

Turn in the armhole edge of each sleeve 1cm (⅜in) and run a gathering thread around the folded edge. Pull up these gathers to fit the armhole edges of bodice, that is, along the outer edge of each shoulder strap and the underarm edge of bodice between ends of each strap. Space out the gathers, drawing most of the fullness to tops of sleeves. Having sleeves and bodice right side out, tack the gathered edges of sleeves in position, just inside the edges of straps and bodice, then top stitch in place along straps and bodice. Now insert elastic in each sleeve casing to fit the child's upper arms. Join ends of elastic and close gaps in the casings.

To make the neck frill

Cut two 10 x 91cm (4 x 36in) strips of large-check fabric. Join the strips at one short end. Narrowly hem one long edge and across short ends. Turn in the remaining long raw edge 2cm (¾in) and press. Now gather along this edge, 1.5cm (⅝in) away from the fold. Pull up gathers to fit bodice around back edges between straps, over straps and across front between ends of straps. Stitch in place through gathers. Stitch ric-rac braid to gathers. Sew a small ribbon bow to centre front of frill.

28

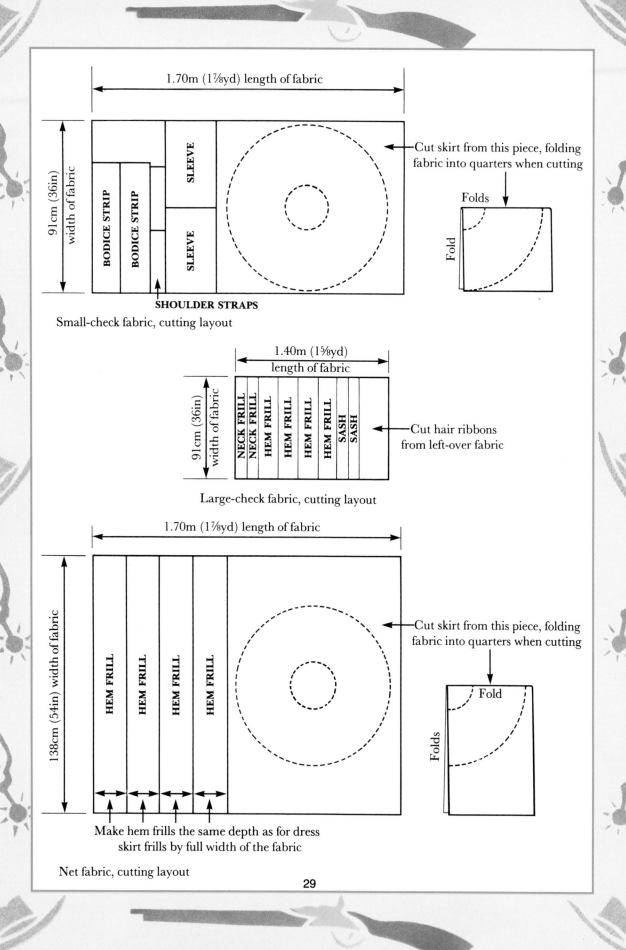

1.70m (1⅞yd) length of fabric

91cm (36in) width of fabric

BODICE STRIP

BODICE STRIP

SLEEVE

SLEEVE

SHOULDER STRAPS

Cut skirt from this piece, folding fabric into quarters when cutting

Folds

Fold

Small-check fabric, cutting layout

1.40m (1⅝yd) length of fabric

91cm (36in) width of fabric

NECK FRILL

NECK FRILL

HEM FRILL

HEM FRILL

HEM FRILL

HEM FRILL

SASH

SASH

Cut hair ribbons from left-over fabric

Large-check fabric, cutting layout

1.70m (1⅞yd) length of fabric

138cm (54in) width of fabric

HEM FRILL

HEM FRILL

HEM FRILL

HEM FRILL

Cut skirt from this piece, folding fabric into quarters when cutting

Fold

Folds

Make hem frills the same depth as for dress skirt frills by full width of the fabric

Net fabric, cutting layout

29

The skirt pattern

Draw the quarter circle skirt pattern onto a large sheet of paper to the measurements given in Diagram 4.

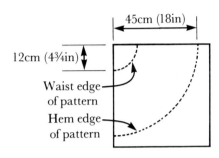

DIAGRAM 4 *drawing the skirt pattern*

To make the skirt

Fold the remaining piece of small-check fabric into quarters and cut out the skirt piece as shown on the cutting layout. This makes a completely circular skirt. Cut the skirt open along one of the fold lines only, for the centre-back seam. Join these edges, taking a 3cm (1¼in) seam and leaving 16cm (6¼in) open at top of seam for back waist opening. Press seam to one side and neaten raw edges of the opening. Narrowly hem lower edge of skirt.

Gather the waist edge of skirt to fit lower edge of the bodice. Stitch in place, having right sides together and raw edges level. Fold the waist seam up against the bodice, then top stitch around bodice just above waist seam, to hold seam in place.

To make the hem frill

Cut four 18 x 91cm (7 x 36in) strips of large-check fabric, or, if frills are to be made deeper, the required depth, by full width of fabric. Join all the strips at short edges to make a continuous length. Narrowly hem one long edge. Turn in the remaining long raw edge 2cm (¾in) and press. Now gather along this edge 1.5cm (⅝in) away from the fold and pull up gathers to fit lower edge of the skirt.

The frill will now be sewn to the lower edge of the skirt with right sides of both uppermost and stitching through the frill gathers. You can adjust the length of the skirt to make it shorter at this stage, by sewing on the frill *above* the hem edge as high up as necessary. Stitch the frill in place, then sew on ric-rac to match the neck frill. Sew fastenings to back edges of bodice and skirt opening.

To make the net underskirt

Trim 2cm (¾in) off the lower edge of the skirt pattern, then cut the skirt and the frill strips as shown in the cutting layout for the net fabric. If you made the frill strips deeper on the skirt, do the same with the net skirt.

Make the underskirt and attach the frill in exactly the same way as for the dress skirt. Gather the waist edge of the underskirt to fit the waist edge of the dress bodice. Catch it to the waist seam on the inside of the dress.

To make the sash

Cut two 10 x 91cm (4 x 36in) strips of large-check fabric. To avoid having a seam at the centre front, cut one strip in half and join one end of each half to the ends of the other strip. Fold strip, bringing the long edges together. Join all the raw edges, leaving a gap for turning. Trim corners of seam, turn right side out and press, then slip stitch gap. Tie in a bow at back of dress when worn.

HAIR RIBBONS

From the remaining strip of large-check fabric, cut two lengths and hem all the raw edges.

Saloon Sal

This dress is made in the same basic way as the Hoe-down gal's dress, except that the sleeves are omitted and the hem frill is added to the skirt so that the lower edge of the frill is just below the hem edge of the dress.

BASIS FOR COSTUME
A pair of slipperettes or suitable shoes
Coloured net tights to match the dress

DRESS, GARTER AND HAIR DECORATION
You will need
1.70m (1⅞yd) of 122cm (48in) wide shiny polyester satin fabric
1.80m (2yd) of 138cm (54in) wide gold or silver lurex net fabric for the dress frills
2m (2¼yd) of 138cm (54in) wide net fabric for the underskirt
2.50m (2¾yd) of narrow braid trimming to match the dress colour
1.30m (1½yd) of 2cm (¾in) wide gold or silver lurex and sequin braid
2.70m (3yd) of marabou feather trimming for the feather boa and hair decoration
A hair-slide

25cm (10in) length of 2cm (¾in) wide elastic for the garter
Fastenings for dress bodice and skirt opening

Note: The quarter circle skirt pattern drawn to the solid line measurements quoted in Diagram 1 will make a finished skirt length of 34cm (13½in) from waist to lower edge of the hem frill. The skirt should be just below knee length on the child. However, the skirt can be made up to 48cm (19in) in length if drawn to the dotted line measurement shown in Diagram 1. For convenience, all amounts of fabric quoted are sufficient to make a dress with a skirt of the maximum length.

The skirt pattern
Draw the quarter circle skirt pattern onto a large sheet of paper to the required measurements as shown in Diagram 1.

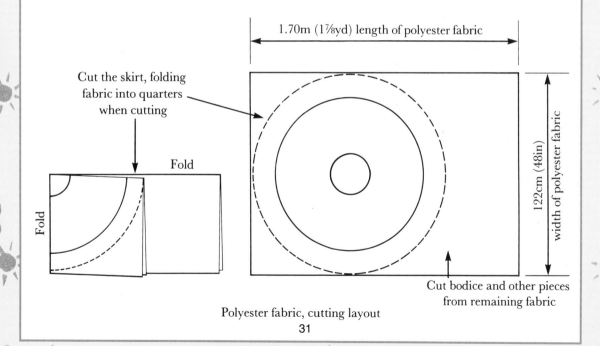

Polyester fabric, cutting layout

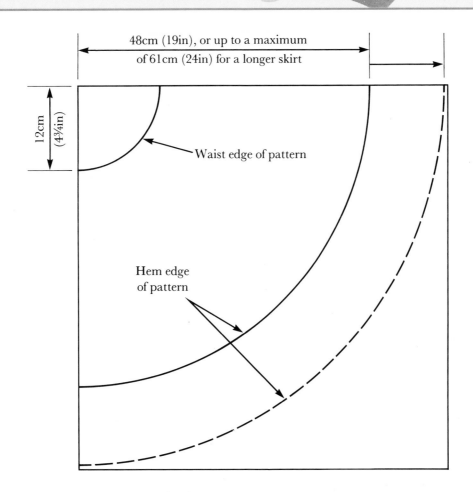

48cm (19in), or up to a maximum
of 61cm (24in) for a longer skirt

12cm (4¾in)

Waist edge of pattern

Hem edge
of pattern

DIAGRAM 1 *the skirt pattern*

To make the skirt
Cut out the skirt as shown on the layout for polyester fabric. Cut the skirt open along one of the fold lines only, for the centre-back seam. Join these edges, taking a 3cm (1¼in) seam and leaving 16cm (6¼in) open at top of seam for back waist opening. Press seam to one side and neaten the raw edges of the opening. Narrowly hem lower edge of the skirt.

To make the skirt frill
Cut four 36cm (14in) wide strips across the full 138cm (54in) width of the lurex net fabric. Join all the strips at short edges to make a continuous length. Fold the strip, right side outside, bringing the long edges together. Press the fold. Gather around the frill, 3cm (1¼in) away from the folded edge. Pull up the gathers so that the frill fits around the skirt on the right side, with the lower edge of the frill just below the hem edge of the skirt. Sew frill to the skirt through the gathers. Stitch the narrow braid trimming along the line of the gathers.

To make the bodice
Using the polyester fabric for all pieces, make the bodice and shoulder straps exactly as given for Hoe-down gal on p26.

To join skirt to bodice
Gather the waist edge of skirt to fit lower edge of the bodice. Stitch in place, having right sides together and the raw edges level. Fold the waist seam up against the bodice, then top stich around the bodice, just above waist seam, to hold the seam in place. Sew fastenings to back edges of bodice and skirt opening.

To make the bodice decoration

Sew a strip of the lurex braid to the upper edge of bodice, between the straps at the front, having ends of braid at centre of positions of straps. Sew centre of the remaining length of lurex braid to centre-front waist edge of bodice. Sew the lengths of braid up the bodice in a V-shape, over the inner edges of shoulder straps and down to the waist edge at the back. Trim off excess length of braid if necessary.

For the bodice frill, cut two 12cm (4¾in) wide strips across the full 138cm (54in) width of the lurex net fabric. Join the strips at one short edge. Fold the strip, right side outside, bringing the long edges together. Press the fold. Gather the frill, 1cm (⅜in) away from the folded edge. Pull up the gathers so that frill fits alongside the outer edge of the lurex braid on the bodice, as shown in the illustration. Stitch the frill in place through the gathers.

Use the remnants of polyester fabric to make three bows as follows. For each bow cut two 7 x 11cm (2¾ x 4¼in) strips of fabric. Join them around the edges, taking a narrow seam and leaving a gap for turning. Turn right side out and slip stitch the gap. Gather up bow tightly at the centre, then fasten off. Sew one bow to waist edge of bodice at centre front and one to the top of each shoulder strap. If desired, make bows for the slipperettes in the same way.

To make the underskirt

Trim 2cm (¾in) off the lower edge of the skirt pattern. Cut the skirt from net fabric, folding the fabric in the same way as shown for the polyester skirt. Now make up the underskirt in exactly the same way as for the dress skirt (see p33).

For the underskirt frill, cut four 18cm (7in) wide strips across the full 138cm (54in) width of the net fabric. Join all the strips at short edges to make a continuous length. Gather round the frill 3cm (1¼in) away from one long edge. Pull up the gathers so that the frill fits around the right side of the underskirt, with lower edge of frill just below the hem edge of the underskirt. Sew frill to the underskirt through the gathers.

Gather the waist edge to fit waist edge of the dress bodice. Catch it to the waist seam on the inside of the dress.

To make the garter

Cut a 7 x 50cm (2¾ x 20in) strip from a remnant of the polyester fabric. Join the long edges of the strip and trim seam, then turn right side out. Thread the length of elastic through, pushing the fabric along the elastic to gather. Stitch ends of elastic to the fabric at each end of the strip.

Now machine stitch along the centre of the garter, stretching the elastic to the full length of the fabric as you go, as in Diagram 2. Lap the

DIAGRAM 2 *stitching along centre of the garter, stretching the elastic as you go*

ends of the garter to fit the child's leg. Sew the lapped ends in place. Cut a 10cm (4in) diameter circle of polyester fabric for the rosette. Turn in raw edge a little and gather round it, then pull up gathers tightly and fasten off. Sew the rosette to garter to cover the join.

To make the hair decoration

Make a couple of small loops from a piece of the marabou trimming and sew all the ends together. Sew these plumes to the hair slide at right angles, so that plumes will stand up above the head when hair-slide is inserted into hair. Use the remainder of the marabou trimming for the feather boa.

Cowboy Kid

The cowboy wears shaggy sheepskin (fur fabric) chaps, constructed just as they would be in real life. The top front edges of the chaps are attached to a belt, but otherwise the legs are completely separate from each other.

BASIS FOR COSTUME

Ordinary checked shirt
Jeans with a belt worn under the chaps
Dark shoes or boots
Ten-gallon hat, toy gun and holster from a
    toyshop
Large handkerchief or scarf, for the neckerchief

CHAPS

You will need
30cm (⅜yd) of 138cm (54in) wide white or
    cream shaggy pile fur fabric*
70cm (¾yd) of 91cm (36in) wide plain brown
    fabric or felt for back portion of the chaps*
10cm (⅛yd) of 91cm (36in) wide leather
    cloth or felt
8 fancy silver buttons about 2cm (¾in) in
    diameter
A buckle with centre bar measuring about 4cm
    (1½in)
Short length of very strong leather thong or
    cord
Adhesive
Metric or imperial graph paper

*Note: The finished inside leg measurement of the chaps is 41cm (16¼in) and the measurement around upper thigh of each chap leg is 42cm (16½in). After making the patterns, try them against the child (wearing jeans) to see if the patterns require lengthening or shortening. Lengthen or shorten both patterns at the ankle edges. If you have lengthened the chaps front pattern more than 10cm (4in), then you will have to buy a piece of fur fabric, the required full length of this pattern.

To make the chaps wider than 42cm (16½in) around the thigh, add the extra required to the inside leg edge of the chaps back pattern. The amount of fabric quoted for the chaps back allows ample for lengthening or

widening as you will see from the cutting layout for these pieces (see pp38-9).

To make
Copy the pattern outlines for the chaps front and back pieces onto graph paper square by square. Test the fur fabric to find the smoothest stroke of the fur pile across the width of fur fabric (or if you have had to buy more fabric, the smoothest stroke along the length).

Referring to the two cutting layouts for the chaps front pieces (according to fabric purchased), pin the pattern to wrong side of fur fabric, taking care that the smooth stroke of pile runs down towards the ankle edge. Cut out the piece, snipping carefully through the backing of fur fabric, so as not to cut through the fur pile on right side.

Turn the pattern over and cut out the second piece in the same way, to make a pair. Turn in the centre front edges of these pieces 1cm (⅜in) and slip stitch in place.

Cut one pair of chaps back pieces from brown fabric or felt, referring to the cutting layout. Turn in the upper edges of these pieces 1cm (⅜in) and stitch down.

Now join each front chaps piece to each back piece at the inside leg edges. Join them also at the outside leg edges from the ankle edges as far as points A shown on the patterns. Reinforce stitching at this point. Turn in the seam allowance on raw edges of chaps fronts above point A and slip stitch in place.

For the chaps belt, cut two 45cm (18in) long strips of leather cloth, making the width of the strips the measurement of centre bar of the buckle. If you are using felt for the belt, make the strips from double thickness for strength and tack the thicknesses together.

Turn 2cm (¾in) at one end of each belt strip to wrong side and glue down securely.

Make three holes, in each of these ends, spacing them evenly (see Diagram 1).

To fix the belt to the chaps, lap and pin the belt pieces 1cm (⅜in) over the upper edges of fur fabric as shown in Diagram 1, letting the belt ends with holes extend 1cm (⅜in) beyond chaps pieces at centre front.

At this stage, try the chaps on the child. The chaps belt should be below the jeans belt and you may need to trim a little off the upper edges of fur fabric for a small child. Check the belt length also and trim off any excess length after leaving enough to fasten the belt. Cut the end of one belt strip to a V-point and make holes at intervals as shown in Diagram 1.

Stitch the belt pieces to upper edges of fur fabric as pinned, then continue the stitching all round the edges of each belt strip. Sew the buckle to the end of belt as indicated in Diagram 1.

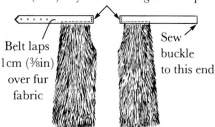

Let these short ends of belt extend 1cm (⅜in) beyond front edges of chaps

Belt laps 1cm (⅜in) over fur fabric

Sew buckle to this end

DIAGRAM 1 *positioning the chaps belt pieces*

Now use the length of leather thong or cord to lace the belt pieces tightly together through the holes at front, then knot the ends securely. Sew the buttons to the belt pieces at regular intervals as shown in the illustration.

Turn in ankle edges of the chaps 1cm (⅜in) and slip stitch in place.

WAISTCOAT

You will need

30cm (⅜yd) of 91cm (36in) wide leather cloth or felt*

2.20m (2½yd) of ric-rac braid

4 fancy silver buttons about 2cm (¾in) in diameter

Adhesive

Sticky tape

Metric or imperial graph paper

*Note: The finished waistcoat measures 64cm (25¼in) around the chest and 23cm (9in) from back neck to lower edge. If you need to lengthen the patterns, add the extra to the lower edges and this amount to your fabric requirements. To widen the patterns, add one quarter of the extra to each side edge of front and back patterns. This will make no difference to fabric requirements, see Diagram 2.

To make

Copy the pattern outline for waistcoat back onto graph paper square by square. Copy waistcoat front also as shown on the diagram.

If making the waistcoat from leather cloth, fix the patterns to wrong side with pieces of sticky tape, as shown in Diagram 2, then draw around the edges of patterns and cut out. If making from felt, pin patterns to felt and cut out in the usual way.

Join the waistcoat fronts to back at shoulder and the side edges. If you are using leather cloth, glue seams open. If you are using felt, press seams open. Stitch ric-rac around the outer edges and armhole edges of waistcoat.

For the fringe thongs, cut four V-shaped pieces of leather cloth or felt as shown on the pattern. Sew the buttons to waistcoat fronts, catching the thongs underneath the buttons as shown on the pattern.

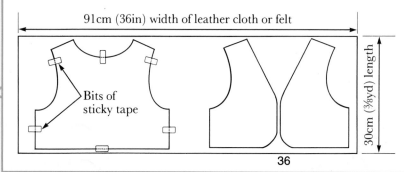

91cm (36in) width of leather cloth or felt

Bits of sticky tape

30cm (⅜yd) length

DIAGRAM 2
cutting the waistcoat pieces

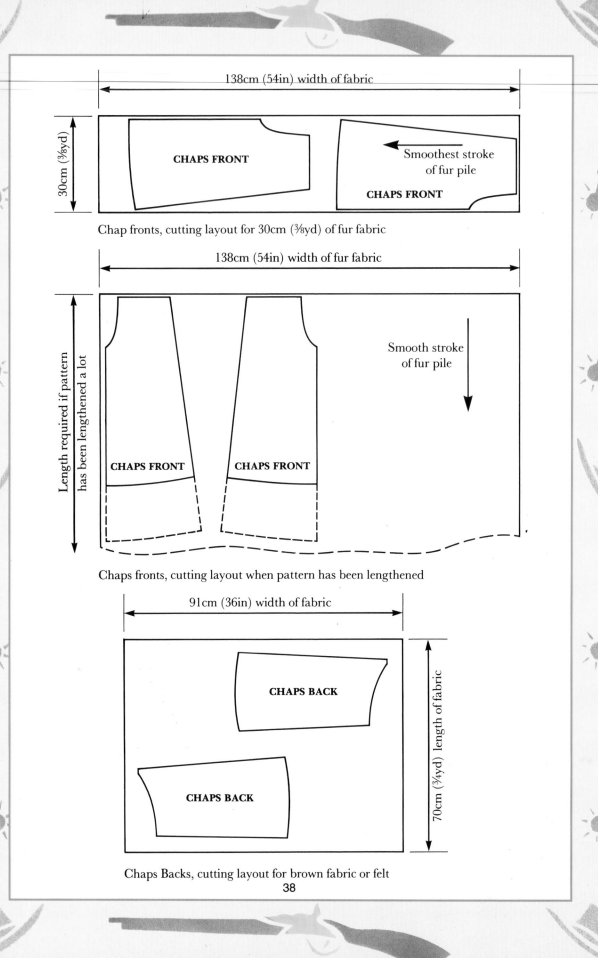

138cm (54in) width of fabric

30cm (⅜yd)

CHAPS FRONT

Smoothest stroke
of fur pile

CHAPS FRONT

Chap fronts, cutting layout for 30cm (⅜yd) of fur fabric

138cm (54in) width of fur fabric

Length required if pattern
has been lengthened a lot

Smooth stroke
of fur pile

CHAPS FRONT

CHAPS FRONT

Chaps fronts, cutting layout when pattern has been lengthened

91cm (36in) width of fabric

CHAPS BACK

CHAPS BACK

70cm (¾yd) length of fabric

Chaps Backs, cutting layout for brown fabric or felt

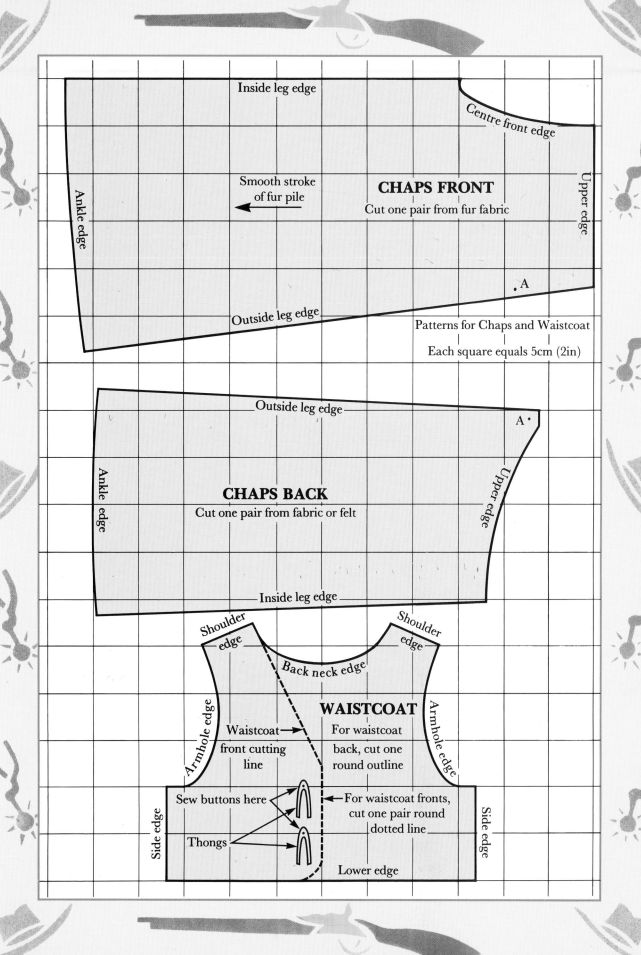

Inside leg edge

Centre front edge

Smooth stroke
of fur pile

CHAPS FRONT
Cut one pair from fur fabric

Ankle edge

Upper edge

.A

Outside leg edge

Patterns for Chaps and Waistcoat

Each square equals 5cm (2in)

Outside leg edge

A .

CHAPS BACK
Cut one pair from fabric or felt

Ankle edge

Upper edge

Inside leg edge

Shoulder edge

Shoulder edge

Back neck edge

Armhole edge

Armhole edge

Waistcoat front cutting line

WAISTCOAT

For waistcoat back, cut one round outline

Side edge

Side edge

Sew buttons here

For waistcoat fronts, cut one pair round dotted line

Thongs

Lower edge

Queen Guinevere

This graceful dress was made from a cast-off evening dress which I found in a thrift (charity) shop. As the skirt was very full, it provided enough material to make the complete dress for a child. The fabric is soft polyester jersey with sparkling silver lurex thread and this type of material or something similar should be used, because it drapes so well and also does not fray.

DRESS

You will need

2.20m (2½yd) of 122cm (48in) wide jersey fabric*

A 30cm (12in) zip fastener

2m (2¼yd) of 2.5cm (1in) wide fancy braid

Metric or imperial graph paper

Note: The dress pattern measures 93cm (37in) in length at the centre from neck to hemline. Although this would appear to be much too long for a small child, after the dress is made up, the hem edge is shortened at the front to ground level, tapering towards the complete length of fabric at the sides to leave the back long.

After making the dress pattern, try it against the child to see if it needs to be lengthened. The pattern should trail on the ground about 10-15cm (4-6in). Lengthen the pattern if required as shown in Diagram 1.

From the cutting layout (Diagram 2) you will see that it is possible to lengthen the hem edge of the dress considerably, if the sleeves are omitted from this layout. In this case, 40cm (½yd) more fabric will be required in order to make the sleeves. Note that the sleeve pattern can be lengthened at the wrist edges as necessary, making no difference to fabric requirements.

The bodice portion of the dress will fit up to a 56cm (22in) chest measurement (allowing for some ease), but the chest size can be adjusted to fit larger sizes. Simply add one quarter of the extra measurement required to the bodice portion of the pattern as shown in Diagram 1.

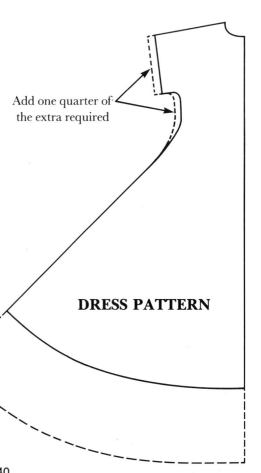

Add one quarter of the extra required

DRESS PATTERN

DIAGRAM 1 *adjusting bodice and lower edge of pattern for larger sizes*

Cutting out

Copy the dress and the sleeve pattern outlines onto graph paper square by square. Adjust patterns if necessary as described.

Before cutting out the dress pieces, cut two 5cm (2in) wide strips across the full 122cm (48in) width of the fabric for the girdle. If you bought extra fabric for the sleeves, cut off this piece also.

Now fold the fabric, bringing the short raw edges together and having selvedges level. Referring to Diagram 2, cut out the dress front, placing pattern to folded edge of fabric. Cut out the dress backs, adding 1cm (⅜in) to long edge when cutting, for seam allowance, as shown in Diagram 2.

Cut the sleeves from the remnants of fabric (or the extra piece), placing the edge of pattern indicated to fold in fabric for each sleeve.

To make

Join centre-back edges of back dress pieces, leaving 31cm (12⅜in) open at the neck edge of seam for inserting the zip fastener. Press

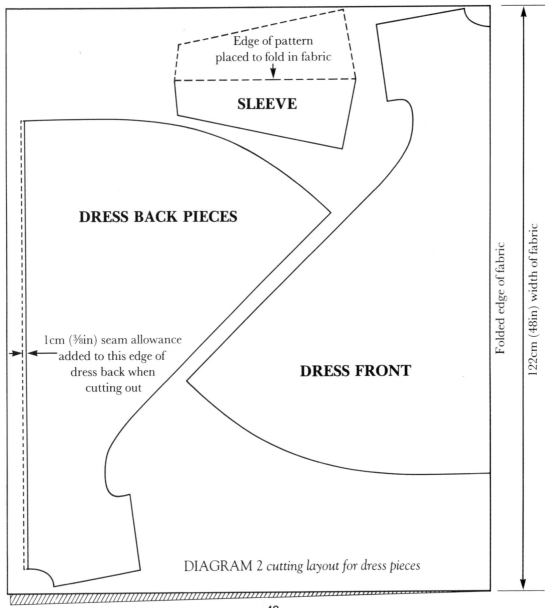

Edge of pattern placed to fold in fabric

SLEEVE

DRESS BACK PIECES

1cm (⅜in) seam allowance added to this edge of dress back when cutting out

DRESS FRONT

Folded edge of fabric

122cm (48in) width of fabric

DIAGRAM 2 *cutting layout for dress pieces*

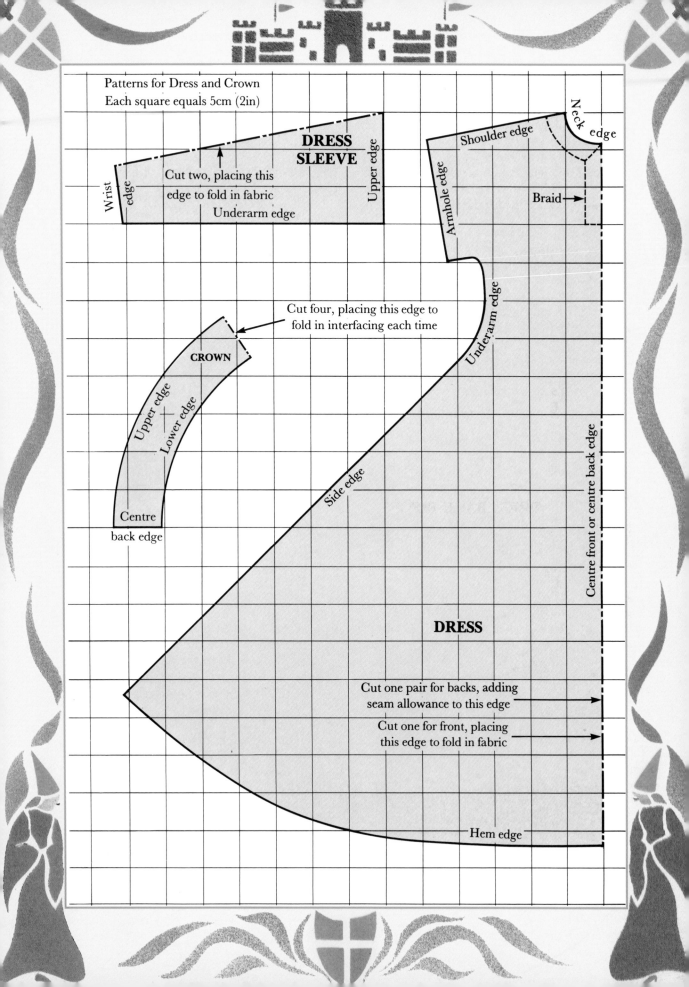

Patterns for Dress and Crown
Each square equals 5cm (2in)

DRESS SLEEVE

Wrist edge

Cut two, placing this
edge to fold in fabric

Underarm edge

Upper edge

Shoulder edge

Neck edge

Armhole edge

Braid →

Underarm edge

Cut four, placing this edge to
fold in interfacing each time

CROWN

Upper edge

Lower edge

Centre
back edge

Side edge

Centre front or centre back edge

DRESS

Cut one pair for backs, adding
seam allowance to this edge →

Cut one for front, placing
this edge to fold in fabric →

Hem edge

seam open. Join dress front to back at the shoulder edges. Clip the curves in neck edge within the seam allowance, then turn in seam allowance and stitch down. Insert the zip fastener at open back edges.

Join dress front to back at the side and underarm edges. Stitch again at underarm curves to reinforce seams, then clip seams at curves. Turn in seam allowance at armhole edges and stitch down. Sew braid around the armhole edges on the right side. Sew braid around the right side of neck edge, easing it around the curves and also sewing it a short way down the centre front of dress as shown on pattern and in illustration, mitring at corners.

Join the underarm edges of each sleeve. Hem lower edges of sleeves and sew on braid. Turn dress and sleeves inside out. Pin the upper raw edges of sleeves to armholes of dress, having the raw edges of sleeves lapping the armholes of the dress 2.5cm (1in). Slip stitch sleeve edges in place.

Put the dress on the child, wrong side out. Turn up and pin hem edge at centre front so that it touches the ground. Continue pinning up the hem, tapering the turn-up towards the side seams of the dress.

Remove the dress, then mark and trim off the excess length at front of dress, allowing for a hem. Hem lower edge.

Join the 5cm (2in) wide girdle strips of fabric at one pair of short edges. Trim to a 2m (2¼yd) length. Join the long edges of the strip and across one short end, taking a narrow seam. Use the knob end of a knitting needle to turn girdle right side out. Turn in short end and slip stitch.

Tie a single knot at each end of the girdle. When the girdle is worn, take the ends from the front to the back, cross over at back and bring to front again then knot, as shown in the illustration.

CROWN AND VEILS
You will need
60cm (⅝yd) of 82cm (32¼in) wide, heavy sew-in interfacing
40cm (½yd) of 91cm (36in) wide gold fabric
1.30m (1½yd) of lurex and sequin braid
3 fruit gums for the jewels

1m (1⅛yd) of 91cm (36in) flimsy transparent fabric for the veil and chin veil
Metric or imperial graph paper
A small safety-pin
Sticky tape
Adhesive

To make the crown
Copy the pattern onto graph paper square by square. Fold a piece of paper and, using the pattern, cut the crown from folded paper, placing edge of pattern indicated to fold in paper. Join centre back edges of crown, butting them together, with a bit of sticky tape.

Now try the crown on the child to see if it needs to be made smaller or larger. No seam allowance is required on the crown, so make it the exact size and then adjust the pattern accordingly at centre back edges.

Cut four crown pieces from the interfacing, placing the edge of pattern indicated to fold in interfacing each time. Apply dots of adhesive to two of the pieces and glue them to the other two pieces. Apply dots of adhesive to these pieces and place them, glued-side down, onto the wrong side of the gold fabric. Cut out the fabric 1cm (⅜in) larger all round than the interfacing pieces. Turn and glue this extra fabric over to the other side of the interfacing, clipping the curves at intervals. Now glue the crown pieces to each other with interfacing sides together. Stitch all round the edges. Bring centre back edges together and oversew neatly to join. Glue braid around the upper and lower edges of the crown. Glue fruit-gums to the front as shown in the illustration.

To make the veils
For the chin veil, cut a 25cm (10in) wide strip across the full 91cm (36in) width of the veil fabric. Trim this strip to measure 76cm (30in). Hem all the raw edges. When worn, the veil is taken under the chin and then the short ends are lapped over each other across the top of the head. The visible short end is then held in place with the safety-pin.

Hem the edges of the remaining piece of veil fabric. Gather along one 91cm (36in) edge. Pull up the gathers to fit back half of the crown at the lower edge. Sew the gathers to inside of the crown, spacing them out evenly.

Artist

A man's old shirt can be transformed into an artist's smock in moments by stitching a few pleats in the shoulders to give the authentic fullness to the garment. The shirt was purchased for next-to-nothing from a thrift (charity) shop, but you may have a suitable one around the house.
You only need to make a huge beret and neck bow, plus a cardboard palette and paint-brush to complete this simple but effective outfit.

BASIS FOR COSTUME
Ordinary trousers and shoes or sandals

SMOCK
You will need
A man's old shirt – any size will do – but it must be regular, loose fitting and not the darted or waisted kind

To make
Trim off the shirt tails (if any) or trim off lower edge of shirt so that it is about knee length on the child. Hem the cut edge.

Put the shirt on the child and button it up. Now pin three pleats on each shoulder of the yoke or shoulder portion of the shirt, having the pleats folding away from the collar and towards the sleeves. The shoulders of the shirt should now fit the child's shoulders; if not, adjust the depth of the pleats accordingly. Stitch the pleats in place on the yoke or shoulder portion as pinned. You can see the pleats clearly in the back view of the outfit.

Trim off the lower edges of the shirt sleeves, leaving the sleeves about 5cm (2in) longer than the child's fingertips. Hem the cut edges. Roll up the sleeves to form cuffs when the smock is worn.

NECK BOW
You will need
A long scarf, or fabric strips, to make an 18 x 150cm (7 x 60in) length

To make
If fabric strips are used, join short edges to make the required length, then hem the outer edges.

Pass the scarf or fabric strip under the shirt collar and tie it in a floppy bow at the front.

BERET
You will need
A 50cm (20in) diameter circle of fabric which should be thin and soft enough to gather up tightly around the edge
50cm (½yd) of 82cm (32¼in) wide, medium iron-on interfacing
1.60m (1¾yd) bias binding to match the fabric
50cm (½yd) narrow elastic
oddment of knitting yarn for the tassel

To make
Cut a 30cm (12in) and a 45cm (17¾in) diameter circle of interfacing and mark the centre on each one. Mark centre of fabric circle on the right and the wrong side. Iron the smaller interfacing circle onto wrong side of fabric circle, matching the centre points. Iron the larger interfacing circle to fabric circle in the same way, over the previous interfacing circle.

Bind the outer edge of the fabric circle with bias binding, leaving a gap for threading through the elastic. Thread the elastic through and join ends to fit child's head. Close the gap. Make a tassel from knitting yarn and sew to marked centre of beret on the right side.

PALETTE AND BRUSH
You will need
Strong card

Brown wrapping-paper
Coloured paper
Scrap of kitchen foil
Length of fawn knitting-yarn
Brown crayon
Poster paints or marker pens
Metric or imperial graph paper
Adhesive

To make the palette

Copy the pattern outline onto graph paper, square by square. Using this pattern, cut the palette shape from card and also cut out the thumb hole. If the card is very thin, cut another one or two and glue them all together so that palette is rigid. Cover both sides of the palette by gluing on brown paper. Shade over the paper with brown crayon to resemble wood grain. Polish the palette with a cloth to remove surplus crayon.

On one side of the palette, paint splodges of poster colour, or use marker pens instead. If desired, paint over each colour with clear nail-varnish, for a wet appearance.

To make the brush

Cut a 25cm (10in) square of coloured paper for the brush handle. Starting at one corner, roll up the paper tightly to form a thin tapered cone-shape, then glue the end in place. Trim off a little at each end of cone to make level.

For the bristles, make a small bunch of yarn strands and tie them together at centres. Fold at centre and glue into the widest end of the brush handle. Spread glue on the ends of the yarn strands and twirl them together to form a point.

Glue a narrow strip of kitchen foil around the handle, just below the bristles. Nip the foil-covered section of the handle to flatten it.

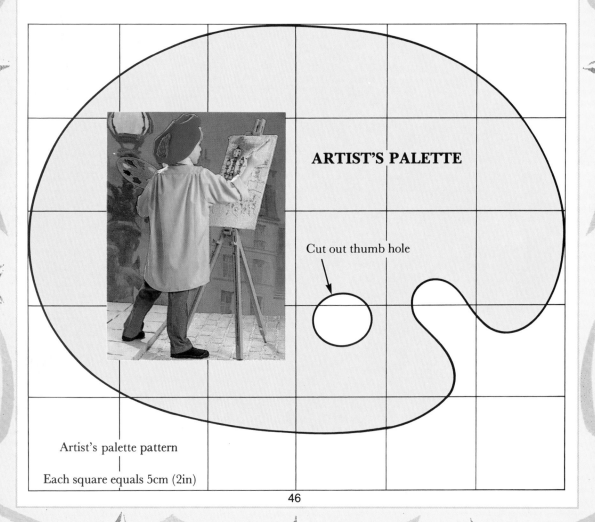

ARTIST'S PALETTE

Cut out thumb hole

Artist's palette pattern

Each square equals 5cm (2in)

Miss Charlotte

This is probably the most elaborate costume in the book, but the end result is so sensational that the cost and effort involved are entirely worthwhile. The dress is made from spotted net fabric which does not fray, so hems are not required on the frills and this saves a lot of stitching. Instructions are also given for making a hooped underskirt to create the authentic crinoline shape. Because the dress is designed with a properly fitted bodice, it could also be made as a very special dress for a little bridesmaid at a wedding.

HOOPED UNDERSKIRT
You will need
2.50m (2¾yd) of 91cm (36in) wide white cotton fabric
7.70m (8⅜yd) of Rigilene*
Fastenings for waistband and shoulder straps

**Note:* Rigilene is polyester boning about 12mm (½in) in width which is sold by the metre (yard) in haberdashery departments of good department stores or at home-sewing and needlecraft suppliers. It is used to make the hoops on the underskirt.

To make
First trim a 20cm (9in) wide strip off one end of the fabric across the full 91cm (36in) width. This piece will be used later for the waistband and the shoulder straps.

Join the short edges of the remaining fabric, leaving 23cm (9in) open at one end of the seam for centre-back waist opening. Press the seam open and neaten raw edges of opening.

Now on the right side of the underskirt, iron three creases at 20cm (8in) intervals above the hem edge as shown in Diagram 1. Fold the fabric at each crease line, having the right side outside as before, then stitch through both thicknesses of fabric 2cm (¾in) away from the fold. Press each of these tucks flat, towards the hem edge.

For the first hoop (at hem edge of the underskirt) cut a 2.30m (2½yd) length of Rigilene. Turn hem edge of fabric 2cm (¾in) to wrong side and press, to form casing for Rigilene. Pin one end of Rigilene inside the casing so that it will not slip through casing as you are stitching. Now stitch hem edge of fabric in place, enclosing the Rigilene strip as you go and taking care not to catch it in the stitching. Before completing the stitching, join the ends of the Rigilene as follows. Lap the ends 2cm (¾in) and hand sew them securely together. Now finish stitching, to enclose the last portion of Rigilene.

For the second hoop, cut a 2.14m (2⅜yd)

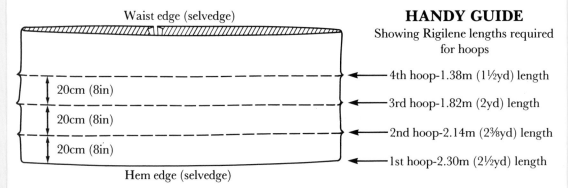

HANDY GUIDE
Showing Rigilene lengths required
for hoops

Waist edge (selvedge)

20cm (8in)

20cm (8in)

20cm (8in)

Hem edge (selvedge)

4th hoop-1.38m (1½yd) length

3rd hoop-1.82m (2yd) length

2nd hoop-2.14m (2⅜yd) length

1st hoop-2.30m (2½yd) length

DIAGRAM 1 *position of creases in the hooped underskirt fabric*

length of Rigilene. Fold the first tuck on the underskirt downwards, forming the casing for Rigilene. Pin end of Rigilene as before, then stitch folded edge of the tuck down, enclosing Rigilene as you go. Join ends as before.

For the third hoop, cut a 1.82m (2yd) length of Rigilene and enclose inside the second tuck, etc as before, but note that because this Rigilene strip is much shorter than the fabric length, you will eventually have to pull it through the casing as you stitch, thus gathering up the fabric as you go.

For the fourth hoop, cut a 1.38m (1½yd) length of Rigilene and stitch in place as for the third hoop. Space out the fabric gathers evenly at third and fourth hoops.

At this stage, the underskirt length is about 77cm (30in), which is suitable for height 110cm (3ft 7in) upwards. For smaller children, the length may have to be trimmed. Gather the waist edge of underskirt to fit the child's waist, then try it on the child. The hem edge should be well clear of the ground. If necessary, mark excess length at the waist edge, pull out the gathers, then cut off the excess.

Gather waist edge to fit child's waist. From the fabric kept aside, cut a 6cm (2½in) wide strip across the 91cm (36in) width of the fabric for the waistband. Use this to bind gathered waist edge, trimming strip to length, but leaving enough for a waistband overlap. Sew fastenings to ends of waistband.

Very small children may require shoulder-strap supports for the underskirt. Make these from fabric strips cut to the required length. Sew one end of each to the waistband at front, then pass them over the shoulders, crossing the straps over at the back. Secure the other ends to waistband with fastenings as desired.

DRESS
You will need

6m (6½yd) of 138cm (54in) wide non-fray white spotted or plain net fabric *

40cm (½yd) of plain white cotton fabric for lining the bodice

3.20m (3½yd) of 91cm (36in) wide dress-lining fabric such as taffeta, for the skirt lining *

A length of 2.5cm (1in) wide red velvet ribbon, the child's waist measurement, plus 6cm (2½in)

A small buckle to suit width of ribbon

40cm (½yd) of narrow elastic

A fancy button or brooch for neck of dress

Fastenings for dress bodice and skirt opening

Metric or imperial graph paper

*Note: The net should be very soft and not the stiff kind which is required for making ballet skirts. Curtain net was used for this dress since it is usually much cheaper than net fabrics which are sold specifically for dressmaking.

The quantities of fabric quoted for the net and skirt lining are sufficient for all sizes. When making the skirt frills for children taller than 100cm (3ft 3in), any adjustment will be

DIAGRAM 2 *the dress-skirt lining pattern*

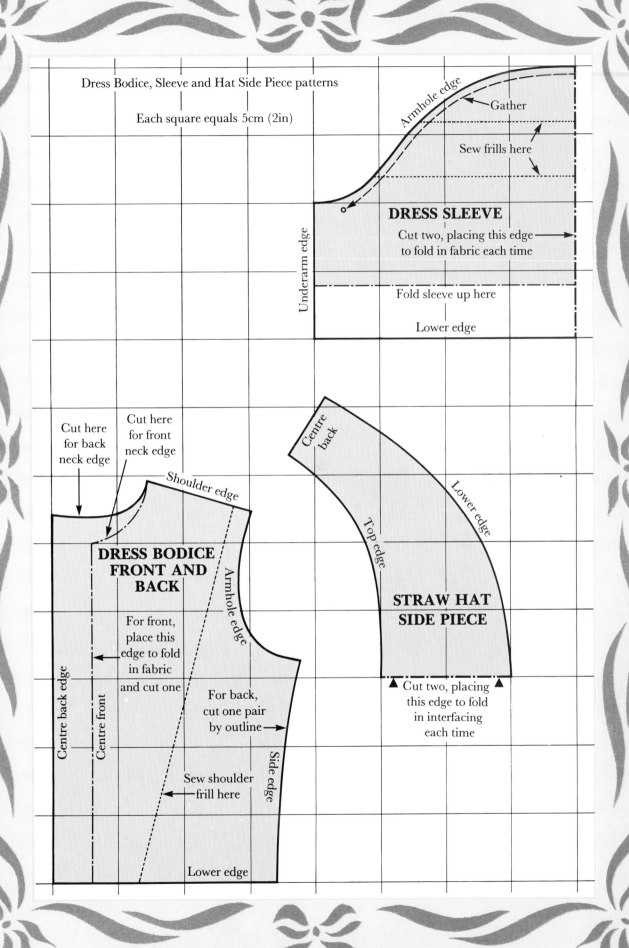

Dress Bodice, Sleeve and Hat Side Piece patterns

Each square equals 5cm (2in)

DRESS SLEEVE

Armhole edge

Gather

Sew frills here

Underarm edge

Cut two, placing this edge to fold in fabric each time

Fold sleeve up here

Lower edge

Cut here for back neck edge

Cut here for front neck edge

Shoulder edge

DRESS BODICE FRONT AND BACK

Armhole edge

For front, place this edge to fold in fabric and cut one

For back, cut one pair by outline

Centre back edge

Centre front

Side edge

Sew shoulder frill here

Lower edge

Centre back

Top edge

Lower edge

STRAW HAT SIDE PIECE

Cut two, placing this edge to fold in interfacing each time

made on the *waist frill*, the other frills are exactly the same for all sizes.

The bodice and sleeve patterns are given on a scaled-down diagram. The sleeve pattern will fit all sizes, but the instructions provide for the enlarging of the bodice pattern if necessary, to fit larger sizes.

The skirt lining (make from taffeta)

First put the hooped underskirt on the child. Measure from the waist over the *curve* of the underskirt down to floor level and take a note of this measurement. To be on the safe side, it is better to be generous with the skirt length since any excess can be trimmed off later on.

Now make the skirt-lining pattern as shown in Diagram 2. There is no need for great accuracy in the measurements, but do take care that you have allowed enough on the length.

Cut four skirt-lining pieces using the pattern and placing pattern to a fold in the taffeta fabric each time as indicated. Join the skirt-lining pieces at the side edges, leaving two of the edges unjoined, for centre-back seam of the skirt as shown in Diagram 3. Since it is easier to sew the frills in place while the skirt lining is flat, the centre-back seam will be joined later on. As you stitch on the frills, leave about 6cm (2½in) at the end of each frill unattached, when you come near to the centre-back edges of the skirt.

Hem the lower edge of skirt lining. Now mark the positions of frills lightly with pencil all along the skirt as shown in Diagram 4.

Cutting the net frills

Diagram 5 shows how to cut the frills from the net fabric. If you are using *spotted* net, simply

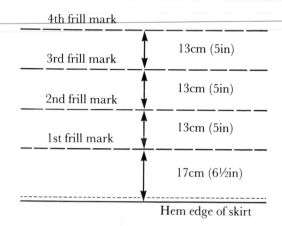

DIAGRAM 4 *marking the positions of frills on the dress-skirt lining*

follow a row of spots when cutting the frill strips. For plain net, use a ruler to measure at intervals as you cut. Cut 1st, 2nd, 3rd and 4th frills all 18cm (7in) wide and to the lengths given in the diagram. *Do not* cut the 5th frill at this stage.

Sewing on the frills

Gather the frills at one long edge so that finished length of each one is about 3m (3¼yd). Stitch each one to the marked line on the skirt.

Fitting the skirt

Now gather the waist edge of the skirt to fit the child's waist. Try it on the child, over the hooped underskirt, pinning the back waist edges together. The 1st skirt frill should just touch the ground. If the skirt is too long, pull out waist gathers and cut excess length off the waist edge.

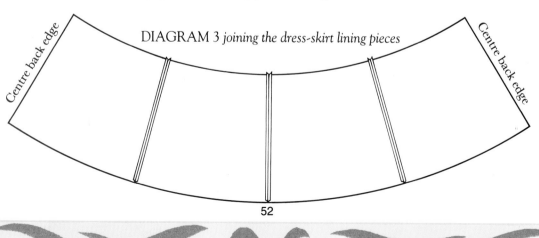

DIAGRAM 3 *joining the dress-skirt lining pieces*

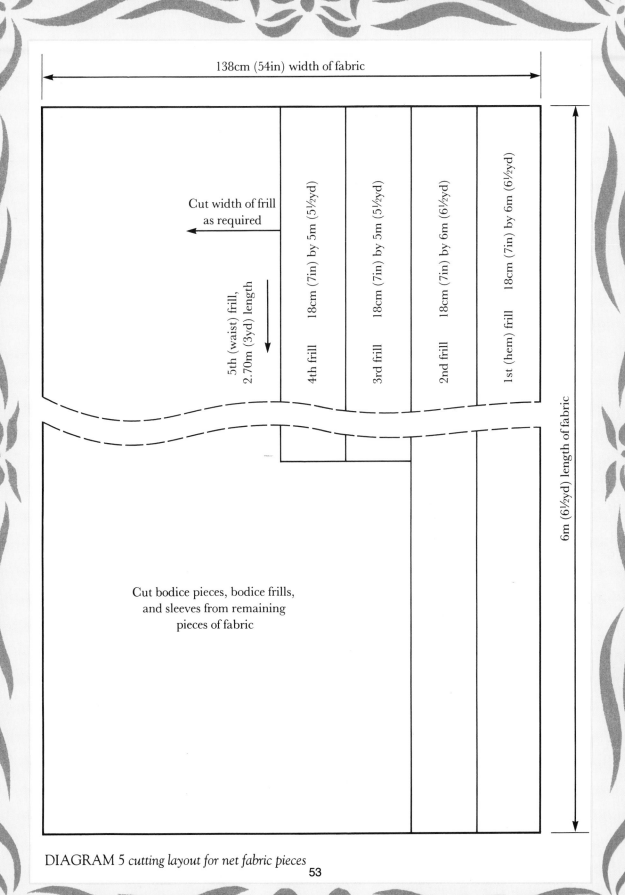

138cm (54in) width of fabric

Cut width of frill
as required

5th (waist) frill,
2.70m (3yd) length

4th frill   18cm (7in) by 5m (5½yd)

3rd frill   18cm (7in) by 5m (5½yd)

2nd frill   18cm (7in) by 6m (6½yd)

1st (hem) frill   18cm (7in) by 6m (6½yd)

6m (6½yd) length of fabric

Cut bodice pieces, bodice frills,
and sleeves from remaining
pieces of fabric

DIAGRAM 5 *cutting layout for net fabric pieces*

The 5th frill

This strip of net fabric is not gathered, but is stitched to the waist edge of the skirt which is later on gathered up to fit the bodice. Take a measurement from waist edge of the skirt to 5cm (2in) below the gathered top edge of the 4th frill. This will be the required width of the frill. Cut this frill 2.70m (3yd) in length as shown in Diagram 5, then stitch one long edge to waist edge of skirt with raw edges of both level. Trim off any excess length of the frill strip.

Finishing the skirt

Pin the loose ends of frills out of the way of the centre-back edges of the skirt. Join centre-back edges, taking a 4cm (1½in) seam and leaving 16cm (6¼in) open at waist end of seam for back waist opening. Fold seam to one side and neaten the raw edges of opening. Now join the short ends of each frill and stitch remainder of each of frill gathers to skirt.

The bodice patterns

Copy the bodice back and front patterns and the sleeve pattern onto graph paper square by square, drawing bodice front pattern by the dotted lines shown on diagram.

This bodice pattern fits up to a 60cm (23½in) chest, and a 52cm (20½in) waist size. The back neck to waist measurement is 25cm (10in). If you need a larger size of bodice, enlarge the pattern as shown in Diagram 6. To ensure a perfect fit, you can now cut the bodice front and back pieces from any oddment of fabric using the adjusted patterns. Join the side and shoulder seams, then try the bodice on the child. Make any adjustments to the bodice patterns. The sleeve pattern fits all sizes.

To make the bodice

Cut bodice front and one pair of backs from net fabric as directed on patterns. Join front to backs at shoulder and side edges. Trim all seams. Now make bodice lining in the same way using the cotton fabric.

Join the lining to bodice around the neck and along the centre-back edges. Trim seams and clip curves at neck edges. Turn right side out. Tack lower edges of lining and bodice together and armhole edges also. Press bodice.

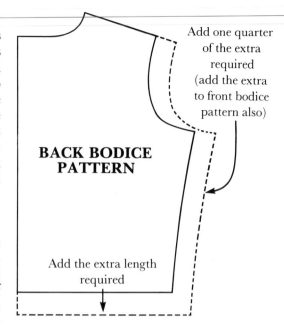

Add one quarter of the extra required (add the extra to front bodice pattern also)

BACK BODICE PATTERN

Add the extra length required

DIAGRAM 6 *enlarging the bodice pattern*

Collar frill

Cut a 4 x 70cm (1½ x 27in) strip of net fabric. Gather one long edge to fit neck edge of bodice. Stitch gathered edge of frill just inside neck edge of bodice.

Centre-front bodice frill

Cut a 4 x 60cm (1½ x 23in) strip of net fabric. Gather down centre of the strip to fit centre front of bodice. Stitch frill in place, turning the collar frill down onto the bodice at neck and lapping the centre frill over it.

To make the sleeves

Cut two sleeves from net fabric, placing pattern to fold in fabric each time as indicated.

For the sleeve frills, cut four 5 x 60cm (2 x 23in) strips of net. Gather one long edge of each frill to fit across sleeves at approximate positions shown on sleeve pattern. Stitch gathered edges in place.

Fold lower edges of sleeves to inside on the fold line shown on the pattern. Stitch edges in place. Stitch again, 1cm (⅜in) away from first stitching line to form casing for the elastic. Thread elastic through to fit child's upper arms and secure elastic at ends of casings.

Join underarm edges of each sleeve. Gather

armhole edges of sleeves between dots as shown on pattern. Sew armholes of sleeves into armholes of bodice, pulling up sleeve gathers to fit, and having right sides together and raw edges level. Stitch again, just within first lines of stitching, then trim seams.

Shoulder frills

Cut two 4 x 120cm (1½ x 47in) strips of net. Gather one long edge of each strip to fit over the shoulders from waist at the front to waist at the back, as shown by dotted line on bodice pattern. Stitch gathered edges of frills in place.

To assemble bodice and skirt

Gather the waist edge of skirt to fit the lower edge of bodice. Stitch in place with right sides together and raw edges level. Fold seam up towards bodice and stitch through bodice at waist edge to hold seam in place.

Slip the buckle onto the length of ribbon and place buckle at centre-front waist edge of the dress bodice. Slip stitch the long edges of ribbon in place around waist of bodice, turning ends to wrong sides of bodice at centre back edges, trimming off any excess length.

Sew fastenings to back edges of the bodice and skirt opening. Add the button or brooch to neck edge of dress.

HAT

You will need

90cm (1yd) of 82cm (32¼in) wide heavy sew-in interfacing
90cm (1yd) of 91cm (36in) wide cream-coloured fabric (to resemble straw)
1.40m (1½yd) of 5cm (2in) wide red ribbon
Metric or imperial graph paper
Adhesive*

*Note: When making the hat, the pieces can be tacked together instead of gluing, although gluing is quicker.

To make

For the hat brim, cut two 44cm (17in) diameter circles from the interfacing. Cut a 17cm (6¾in) diameter circle from the centre of each one and discard them. This size of centre hole will fit head size 53cm (21in) in circumference. Try one piece on the child's head, noting that the finished hat fits on the back of the head as shown in the illustration. Cut the inner circles larger if necessary.

Put dots of glue sparingly here and there on the brim pieces and place them glued-side down on the wrong side of the cream-coloured fabric. Cut out the fabric 1cm (⅜in) away from the inner and outer edges of both brim pieces. Clip the inner edges of fabric, then turn and stick the 1cm (⅜in) extra fabric over to the other side of interfacing at the outer and inner edges. Place the brim pieces together with interfacing on the inside and using dots of glue to hold them together. Machine stitch all around the outer edge of brim, then continue stitching round and round in a spiral towards centre circle, spacing stitching line about 1cm (⅜in).

Draw the hat side-piece pattern outline onto graph paper. If the centre hole of the brim was enlarged, you will need to add extra length to the centre-back edge of this pattern. Add a generous amount, so that the interfacing can be trimmed to length.

Cut two side pieces from interfacing, placing the edge indicated to fold in interfacing each time. Put hat brim on the child, then fit one of the side pieces onto this, lapping back edges as necessary. Trim off excess, noting that the back edges will be butted together, not overlapped. Cover the two interfacing pieces with fabric in the same way as for the brim, then glue them together with interfacing sides inside. Join the centre-back edges by oversewing them neatly together. Stitch this piece in the same way as for the brim, spiralling the stitching from lower to top edge. Oversew the lower edge of the hat side piece to the inner hole of the brim.

The hat top piece is a circle. If the side piece was enlarged, then cut the circle to fit as required. If the side piece is the same size as in the diagram, the circle will be 12cm (4¾in) in diameter. Cut two of the circles from interfacing. Cover with fabric and complete as for the other hat pieces. Oversew the circle to top edge of the hat side piece.

Cut the ribbon into two lengths and sew one end of each length to the sides of hat at inner edge of the brim.

Dick Turpin

For this costume, ordinary wellington boots can be transformed into smart riding-boots of the period, by adding a cuff of tan leather cloth to the tops. If a suitable leather belt is available, use this instead of making one.

BASIS FOR COSTUME
Light brown or fawn trousers or jeans
Ordinary white shirt
Black wellington boots
A red scarf
Three-cornered hat and flintlock gun from a
   toyshop

BOOT CUFFS AND BELT
You will need
Oddments of tan leather cloth or felt
A buckle
Double-sided sticky tape or adhesive

To make the belt
Cut a strip of leather cloth or felt wide enough to fit the buckle and long enough to suit the child. Attach one end to the buckle and make holes at intervals in the other end.

To make the boot cuffs
Cut two 9cm (3½in) wide strips of leather cloth or felt, long enough to go round top edges of the boots, plus 1cm (⅜in). Join the short edges of each strip, taking a tiny seam. Glue the seams open.

   Now cut 1cm (⅜in) deep V-shaped notches all along one edge of each cuff. These edges will be fixed inside the top edges of the boots. If you wish to fix them in place temporarily, place strips of double-sided tape all round the inside of top edges of boots.

   Place the cuffs right side out on the boots, having the notched edges extending 2cm (¾in) above the top edges of the boots with cuff seams at centre back. Turn notched edges to insides of boots and fix to the sticky tape or glue in place.

SLEEVELESS JERKIN
You will need
50cm (⅝yd) of 91cm (36in) wide tan
   non-woven curtain fabric or felt*
Metric or imperial graph paper

*Note: After making the jerkin pattern, try it against the child to see if the length requires adjustment. It should be about hip length on the child. If the lower edge needs to be lengthened, then add this amount to fabric requirements. The width of the jerkin is generous enough to fit most sizes since it is worn open at the front.

To make
Copy the jerkin pattern outline onto graph paper square by square. Adjust length of pattern if necessary as described.

   Fold the fabric, bringing the selvedges together. Place the edge of pattern indicated to the fold and cut the back piece. Now trim the pattern along the front edge as shown by dotted cutting line. Cut the front pieces from remaining double fabric, using this pattern.

   Join the fronts to back at the shoulder edges, then the side edges. Clip curves within seam allowance at neck and armhole edges. Turn in and stitch down armhole edges, then all the outer and neck edges.

CAPE
You will need
2m (2¼yd) of 91cm (36in) wide dark grey or
   black fabric*
A large hook and eye
40cm (½yd) of black bias binding

*Note: Instructions are given for making the cape in two lengths. Cut the shorter length for height up to 110cm (3ft 7in) and the longer

length for taller children. The same amount of fabric will make both sizes. The collar pattern is the same for both sizes.

To make the patterns

For the collar, make a 56cm (22in) diameter circular pattern with a 12cm (4¾in) diameter circle cut out of the centre, for the neck edge.

The cape pattern is a quarter circle. First draw a 72cm (28in) *radius* quarter circle for the small size, or 80cm (31in) *radius* for the larger size. For the neck edge, draw a 10cm (4in) radius quarter circle. You can see this pattern with measurements in the cutting layout.

To make

Cut out the collar first as shown on the cutting layout. Fold the remaining fabric as shown on the layout, then cut out the cape, using the quarter circle pattern as shown.

Cut once through the collar for centre front edges (see layout). Turn in and stitch down seam allowance on the edges of the collar and the cape also, except for the neck edges.

Tack neck edges of cape and collar together, having right sides of both uppermost, raw edges level, and easing the neck edge of collar to fit neck of cape. Stitch as tacked. Clip neck edges within the stitching line.

Fold the neck edge seam allowance down to the inside of the cape. Lift up the collar, then stitch seam allowance to cape. To cover these neck raw edges, sew on bias binding.

Turn the centre front edges of the collar, just inside the hemmed front edges of the cape, then slip stitch them in place. Sew the hook and eye to front corners at neck of cape to fasten.

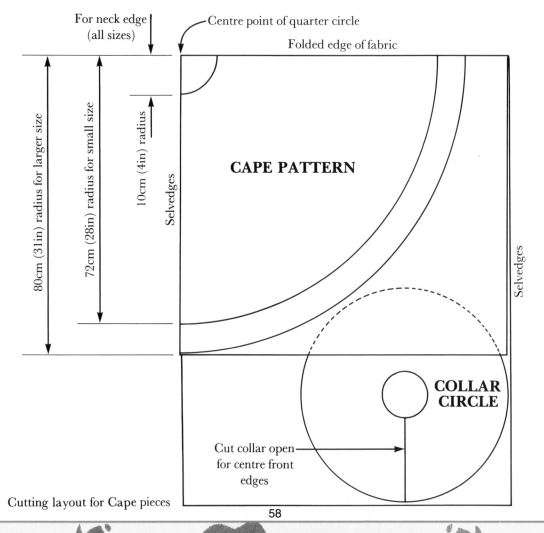

For neck edge (all sizes)

Centre point of quarter circle

Folded edge of fabric

80cm (31in) radius for larger size

72cm (28in) radius for small size

10cm (4in) radius

Selvedges

CAPE PATTERN

Selvedges

COLLAR CIRCLE

Cut collar open for centre front edges

Cutting layout for Cape pieces

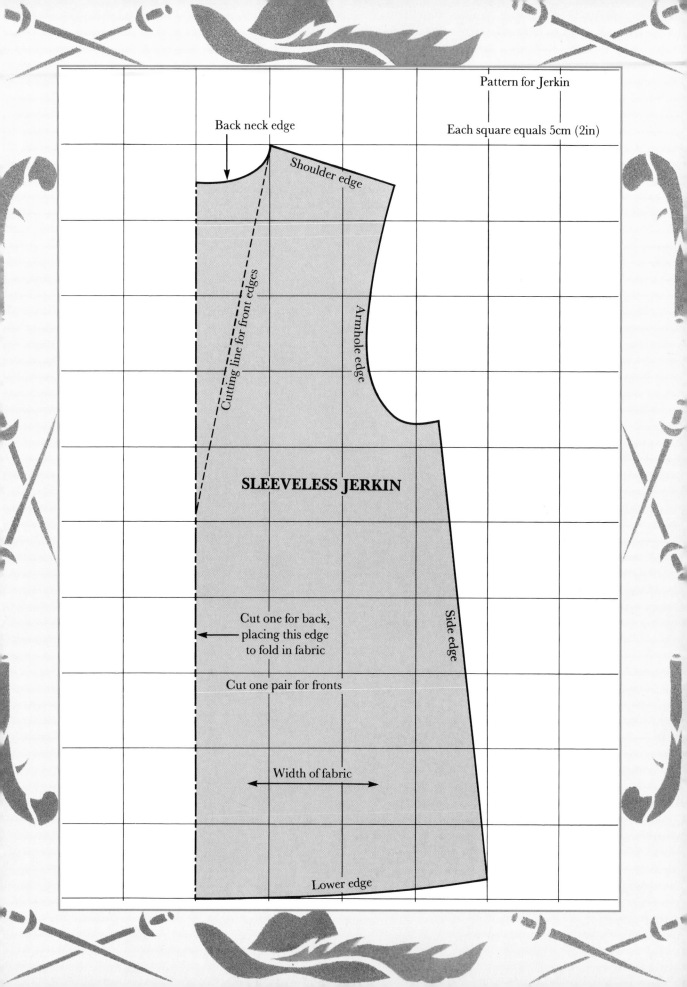

Pattern for Jerkin

Each square equals 5cm (2in)

Back neck edge

Shoulder edge

Armhole edge

Cutting line for front edges

SLEEVELESS JERKIN

Side edge

Cut one for back,
placing this edge
to fold in fabric

Cut one pair for fronts

Width of fabric

Lower edge

Caesar

In reality, the Roman toga would have been a single piece of fabric arranged around the body. For ease of wear, the toga for this costume is made in two pieces: a skirt, and a long strip which is fixed to the left shoulder of the T-shirt with Velcro. Both pieces are straight strips of fabric which were made from an old cotton bed-sheet purchased from a thrift (charity) shop.

BASIS FOR COSTUME
A short-sleeved T-shirt and suitable sandals

TOGA
You will need
An old white sheet, single or double size
4m (4⅜yd) of 4cm (1½in) wide purple ribbon
1.50m (1⅝yd) narrow white tape
A 10cm (4in) length of Velcro

To make
For the skirt, cut a 160cm (63in) long strip off the length of the sheet, making the *width* of the strip the waist to floor measurement on the child. Hem one long edge of the strip and sew on a length of ribbon above the hem.

Join the short edges of the skirt, leaving an 8cm (3in) gap at the top of the seam. Press the seam open and stitch down the raw edges of the gap. Hem the remaining raw edge, forming the casing for the tape. Thread the tape through the casing. Pull the tape ends to gather up the fabric and tie tapes at back of child when the skirt is worn.

For the shoulder strip, cut a 90 x 132cm (36 x 52in) piece off the length of the sheet. Hem all the raw edges. With right side of strip facing you, stitch the ribbon just above the lower long edge and up the right-hand side short edge, mitring the ribbon at the bottom right-hand corner.

Cut a 5cm (2in) length of furry Velcro and of hooked Velcro also. Having the right side of the fabric strip facing you as before, stitch the hooked Velcro strip to top left-hand corner as shown in Diagram 1. This will be called strip A. Stitch the furry Velcro strip to the *wrong* side of top left-hand corner as shown in Diagram 1 also. This will be called strip B.

Sew the remaining 5cm (2in) long strip of hooked Velcro to the left-hand shoulder of the T-shirt in the position shown in Diagram 2.

Put the T-shirt on the child. Having the child's back towards you and right side of fabric strip facing you, attach the *furry* Velcro strip B at corner of fabric to the hooked strip on the T-shirt. Take the fabric strip down across the child's back and pass it under the right arm. Fold the long edge of fabric about 8cm (3in) to the outside as it passes under the arm. Take this folded edge up across the front to drape over the child's left shoulder and hang down the back. Arrange the fabric in a few deep tucks on the shoulder and pin the tucks in place. Remove the fabric strip and hand-sew the tucks in place on the wrong side as pinned, taking care that stitches do not show on the right side.

Finally, sew the remaining 5cm (2in) long strip of furry Velcro across the tucks on the wrong side, so that this Velcro strip can be attached to the hooked Velcro strip A, on the piece of fabric.

Hooked
Velcro strip

Front of T-shirt

DIAGRAM 2 *positioning the hooked velcro strip on left-hand shoulder of T-shirt*

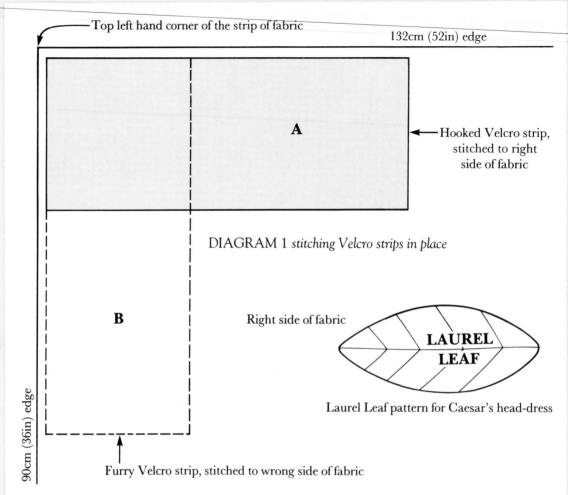

Top left hand corner of the strip of fabric

132cm (52in) edge

A

Hooked Velcro strip, stitched to right side of fabric

DIAGRAM 1 *stitching Velcro strips in place*

B

Right side of fabric

90cm (36in) edge

Furry Velcro strip, stitched to wrong side of fabric

LAUREL LEAF

Laurel Leaf pattern for Caesar's head-dress

LAUREL HEAD-DRESS

You will need
Small pieces of metallic gold gift wrapping-paper (the kind with a paper backing, not foil)
Small pieces of brown wrapping-paper
1.20m (1⅜yd) of 1.5cm (⅝in) wide, gold ribbon
Adhesive such as UHU
Water-soluble adhesive suitable for sticking paper

To make
Using water-soluble adhesive, glue the gold paper to the brown paper and leave to dry. Trace the laurel leaf pattern off the page and use this to cut out twenty-five leaves from the gold paper. Using the point of a darning needle, mark the veins on each leaf as shown on the pattern. Bend the sides of each leaf up slightly, folding at the centre vein.

Use UHU-type adhesive when gluing the leaves to the ribbon. At the centre of the length of ribbon, glue on one leaf horizontally. Now glue on the remaining leaves in equal pairs on either side of this leaf, lapping each pair about 1.5cm (⅝in) over the previous pair. (See the illustration, which shows the arrangement of leaves quite clearly.)

When the head-dress is worn, tie the ribbon ends in a bow at the back of the child's head.

SCROLL

You will need
A 25 x 40cm (10 x 16in) strip of heavy white sew-in interfacing
Oddment of red ribbon

To make
Roll up the strip of interfacing along the length and tie the ribbon around it in a bow.

Cleopatra

*Cleopatra's dress is simply a tube of fabric held up with shoulder straps.
Instructions are given for making the wig from chunky black knitting yarn, but this
can be omitted if the child has dark hair, in which case only a headband would
be required. The gold collar and bracelets are fashioned from metallic gift
wrapping-paper glued on to firm interfacing for extra durability.*

BASIS FOR COSTUME

A pair of flip-flops or other sandals, which can
  be painted gold if desired

A small vase and a toy snake from a toyshop
  for the asp

DRESS AND CAPE

90cm (1yd) of 152cm (60in) wide polyester
  jersey fabric*

4.20m (4⅝yd) of narrow trimming or ribbon

2m (2¼yd) of gold dressing-gown cord

50cm (½yd) of narrow elastic

*Note: From this width and amount of fabric,
the underarm to hem edge of the dress can be
made up to about 84cm (33in) in length. The
dress should be ankle-length on the child. If a
longer dress length is required, the most
economical way is to buy 91cm (36in) wide
fabric and calculate the amount needed by
referring to Diagram 1. The 90cm (1yd)
measurement on the diagram would become

the *width* of your fabric, so add the collar
diameter to the dress length required and this
will be the necessary amount of fabric.

To make the cape

Cut a 66cm (26in) diameter circle from the
fabric as shown in Diagram 1, or from one end
of the fabric if you are using 91cm (36in) wide
fabric. Cut a 16cm (6¼in) diameter circle
from the centre and discard it. Fold the cape in
half and trim off the shaded portion as shown
in Diagram 2, thus forming points for the knot-

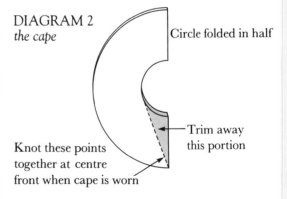

DIAGRAM 2
the cape

Circle folded in half

Trim away
this portion

Knot these points
together at centre
front when cape is worn

ted front fastening. Sew on the trimming or
ribbon around the edges. If you are using fabric
which frays, hem the raw edges before stitching on the trimming or ribbon.

To make the dress

Cut a strip off the remaining piece of fabric as
shown in Diagram 1, making the width of this
strip (or *length* of the strip if using 91cm (36in)
wide fabric), the child's underarm-to-floor
measurement. In either case the 90cm (36in)
measurement goes *around* the child.
  Join the other edges of the strip for the

152cm (60in) width of fabric

Make this the child's underarm
to floor measurement

90cm (1yd)

DRESS

CAPE

DIAGRAM 1 *cutting out the dress and cape*

centre-back seam of the dress. Hem one remaining 90cm (36in) raw edge to form a casing for the elastic, leaving a gap in the stitching. Thread the elastic through to fit around the child's chest under the arms. Join ends of elastic and close gap in stitching. Make two narrow shoulder straps from remnants of the fabric. Sew the ends to the wrong side of front and back of the dress, adjusting the length as necessary to hold dress up closely under arms.

The lower edge of the dress should now be ankle length. Trim off any excess length if necessary, then sew on the trimming or ribbon. If using fabric which frays, hem raw edge before stitching on trimming or ribbon.

Knot the dressing-gown cord 5cm (2in) away from each end, then fray out the ends. Take it around the waist from front to back, cross over at the back, bring to front again, then knot, as shown in the illustration.

COLLAR AND BRACELETS
You will need
A sheet of metallic gold gift wrapping-paper (the kind with a paper backing, not foil)
Oddments of two other colours of similar metallic paper
35cm (14in) of 82cm (32¼in) wide heavy sew-in interfacing
A 16cm (6¼in) length of Velcro
2.20m (2½yd) of narrow gold cord or braid
Adhesive such as UHU
Water-soluble adhesive for sticking paper

To make the collar
Draw a 34cm (13½in) diameter circle onto a piece of interfacing. Mark the centre, then cut out the circle. Draw a 13cm (5in) diameter circle at the centre, but do not cut out at this stage. Using the UHU-type adhesive, glue the unmarked side of the circle to the wrong side of the gold paper. Cut out the paper level with the outer edge of the interfacing circle.

Push a pin through the marked centre of the interfacing to mark the centre of the paper circle. With paper side uppermost, draw a 19cm (7½in) and a 26cm (10¼in) diameter circle onto the paper. Now use a blunt pencil to rule two lines right across the gold paper through the centre, to divide the circle into quarters. Scribble on one quarter to mark it as the one

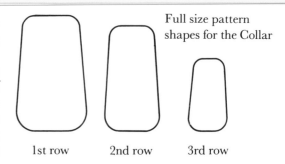

Full size pattern shapes for the Collar

1st row   2nd row   3rd row

which will be cut away later on. Continue drawing lines across the circle to divide each quarter into eight equal sections.

Now cut away the scribbled quarter and also the innermost circle as marked on the interfacing side of the collar. Glue the gold cord all around the edges of the collar using UHU-type adhesive.

Using each of the three pattern shapes given for the collar, cut twelve of each from one coloured metallic paper and twelve of each from the other. Glue the shapes to the collar within the marked section, alternating the colours as shown in the illustration, and using the water-soluble adhesive. Wipe off any glue smears with a damp cloth. When the glue is dry, use a blunt pencil to draw around each shape, at the edge and just within the edge.

Cut two 3cm (1⅛in) long strips of hooked Velcro and of furry Velcro. Glue them to the wrong side of the collar as shown in Diagram 3, using UHU-type adhesive. Note that a preliminary coating of glue is advisable on the Velcro pieces and this should be allowed to dry before finally sticking them to the collar. Leave until quite dry before attempting to fasten the Velcro strips.

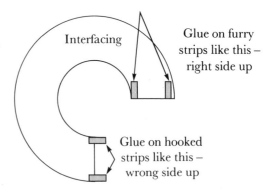

Interfacing

Glue on furry strips like this – right side up

Glue on hooked strips like this – wrong side up

DIAGRAM 3 *gluing the velcro strips*

To make the two bracelets

For one bracelet cut a 5 x 16cm (2 x 6¼in) strip of interfacing. Cut two 1cm (⅜in) long strips of furry Velcro and two 2.5cm (1in) long strips of hooked Velcro. Sew them to the ends of the bracelet strip as shown in Diagram 4.

Sew on furry strips like this – right side up

Sew on hooked strips like this – wrong side up

DIAGRAM 4 *sewing the velcro strips to the bracelet*

Fasten Velcro strips, having them on the inside of the bracelet.

Cut a 5 x 17cm (2 x 6¾in) strip of gold paper. Use a blunt pencil to rule lines across the narrow width of the strip, at 1cm (⅜in) intervals. Now keeping the interfacing bracelet fastened, use UHU-type adhesive to glue the strip of paper to the bracelet. Trim off any excess length. Keeping bracelet fastened, glue gold cord all round edges to match collar.

WIG

You will need

50g (1¾oz) of chunky black knitting yarn*
2m (2¼yd) of narrow gold cord or braid
70cm (¾yd) of 2.5cm (1in) wide gold ribbon
Oddment of heavy sew-in interfacing
A 30cm (12in) diameter circle of black
    stretchy fabric
Adhesive

*Note: When required, straighten out the strands of yarn as follows: use a steam iron on the highest steam setting, hold the iron above the yarn strands for a few moments, then shake the strands.

To make

For the headband, cut two 2.5cm (1in) wide strips of interfacing, long enough to go around the child's head from forehead to back, plus 3cm (1¼in). Glue the strips together forming a double thickness. Mark a 13cm (5in) long section at the centre of one long edge. Leave

this portion uncovered when sewing on the yarn strands, to form the gap for the face.

Now cut a few 50cm (20in) lengths of yarn. Fold them in half and, starting at one end of the interfacing strip, stitch folded ends in place just above one long edge, so that yarn strands hang down below this edge. Continue cutting and sewing on the strands of yarn until the strip is completed, except for the face gap. Steam the yarn strands as described, then trim the ends level.

Place the headband around the child's head, having the looped ends of yarn against the head. Lap and pin the ends of the headband at the back of the head as necessary, to fit loosely. Sew ends of headband as pinned.

For the top portion of the wig, place the circle of black fabric on top of the child's head, then push on the headband over it in the position shown in the illustration. The black fabric circle now has to be trimmed to shape. To do this, first mark the position of the top edge of the headband onto the fabric all round, using a coloured pencil or chalk. Remove the headband and the fabric circle. Cut out the marked shape from the fabric circle, making it 1.5cm (⅝in) larger all round than the markings. The final shape will be an oval, and the centre parting stitching line will run from front to back, that is, along the *length* of the oval.

Cut lengths of yarn to fit across the oval, plus a little extra. Stitch the yarn strands closely together at the centre parting line until the fabric is covered. Steam the yarn strands to straighten them. Spread them out smoothly across the fabric, then stitch in place all around the outer edge of the oval. Trim yarn strands level with the fabric.

Pin the centre-front top edge of the headband to one end of the centre-parting stitching line, lapping the headband over the oval 1.5cm (⅝in). Pin centre back of headband in same way. Pin remainder of headband to the oval, easing the oval to fit. Now slip stitch top edge of headband in place as pinned.

Glue the gold ribbon to the headband, trimming the length to fit. Glue gold cord to the upper and lower edges of the ribbon.

Knot the ends of the remaining length of cord. Tie it into a bow and sew to centre back of headband.

Flower Fairy

All the daisy petals are cut from firm interfacing and the tips are coloured with wax crayon. There are no hems on the petal edges, so this costume can be made up very quickly and it will fit all sizes.

BASIS FOR COSTUME
A yellow short-sleeved T-shirt
Yellow or green tights
A pair of slipperettes or suitable shoes

SKIRT, HAT AND HAND-HELD DAISY
You will need
1.40m (1¾yd) of 82cm (32¼in) wide heavy
    sew-in interfacing
An oddment of yellow fabric for waistband and
    the daisy flower centres
A little stuffing or cotton-wool
A red wax crayon
Paper tissues or paper kitchen-towel, for
    setting the crayon colour into the interfacing
A 6 x 16cm (2¼ x 6¼in) piece of green felt
1m (1yd) of narrow green ribbon
Fastening for waistband

Note: Interfacing usually has the brand name printed along the selvedges. Trim this off the whole length of the interfacing before making a start.

To make the skirt
The skirt is composed of two layers of petals, gathered onto a waistband. The ends of the waistband are joined together when the skirt is worn. For the first layer of petals, cut two 25cm (10in) wide strips across the full *width* of the interfacing. Bring the short edges of *one* of the strips together to fold it in half, then fold in half again as shown in Diagram 1.

Pin all the layers together as shown in Diagram 2. Cut up the centre of the piece to within 5cm (2in) of the waist edge. Cut up the folded sides of the piece in the same way, as shown in Diagram 2. Round off the short edges of the petals as shown in the diagram also. Now fold and cut the remaining strip of interfacing in the same way.

Remove the pins and unfold the strips. Place a piece of paper under each petal tip and colour the rounded edge with wax crayon, shading heavily at the edge and more lightly above it.

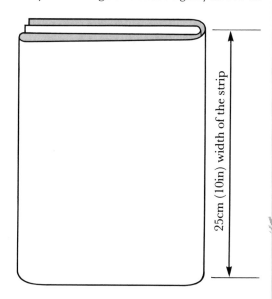

DIAGRAM 1 *folding the skirt interfacing strip*

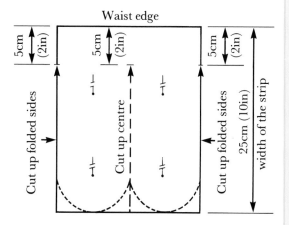

DIAGRAM 2 *cutting the interfacing piece to form the petals*

67

Use a warm iron to press each petal tip between the layers of paper tissue or paper towel. This will set the colour into the interfacing and remove the surplus wax.

Now join the two strips to each other at one end, oversewing the edges together as shown in Diagram 3. Gather the waist edge of the strip to fit around the child's waist.

Make the second layer of petals in the same way from two 25cm (10in) wide strips cut across the width of the interfacing. Gather the waist edge as before. Place the two layers of petals together with coloured sides of petals uppermost and gathered edges level. Stitch through both skirt thicknesses at the gathers.

Cut a 5cm (2in) wide strip of yellow fabric, making the length the child's waist measurement plus 6cm (2½in). Use this to bind the gathered edges of the skirt, letting one end of the strip extend beyond the gathers for the waistband overlap. Sew fastening to ends of the waistband.

To make the hat
Cut two 10 x 55cm (4 x 22in) wide strips across the width of the interfacing. Fold the strips in the same way as for the skirt and cut up the centre and at folds, to within 3cm (1¼in) of the top edges. Colour the petal tips, then gather the long edge of each strip to measure 14cm (6in). Place the layers together and stitch through the gathers as for the skirt. Join the ends of the petal strips by oversewing to form a circle of petals.

For the daisy centre, cut a 16cm (6¼in)

diameter circle of yellow fabric. Gather round the edge, then pull up gathers, stuffing the circle firmly. Pull gathers tightly and fasten off. Place the stuffed circle, gathered side down, at the centre of the daisy petals. Sew the gathered edges of the petals underneath the stuffed circle. Sew the centre of the length of ribbon underneath the hat at the centre. Tie the ribbon underneath the child's hair at the back or under the chin when the hat is worn.

To make the hand-held daisy
Make exactly as for the hat, using two 8 x 40cm (3 x 16in) strips cut across the width of the interfacing. For the daisy centre, use a 12cm (4¾in) diameter circle of yellow fabric.

Use the piece of green felt for the stalk. Join the long edges and across one short end, taking a tiny seam. Turn right side out. Stuff the stalk, then sew the open end underneath the daisy.

WINGS
You will need
A 50cm (20in) square of stiff green net fabric
A 5cm (2in) length of Velcro

To make
Trim each corner of the square to form a curve. Fold the square in half, then gather up the centre and pull up gathers to measure 5cm (2in). Sew the furry Velcro strip to gathers. Sew the corresponding hooked Velcro strip to back of T-shirt, between the shoulder blades.

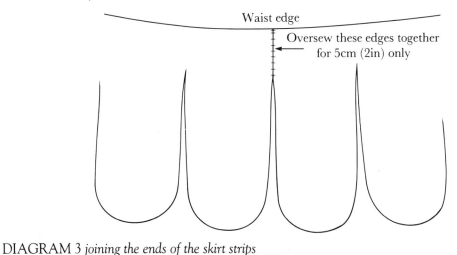

DIAGRAM 3 *joining the ends of the skirt strips*

Circus Clown

This outfit can be made from brightly coloured striped or spotted fabric, or plain shiny satin, with a contrasting colour for the neck frill and rosette trimmings. Whatever fabric you choose, take care that it is soft and thin enough to gather up nicely at the wrists, ankles and neck.

BASIS FOR COSTUME
Slipperettes or suitable shoes
A toy trumpet or other suitable accessory

TUNIC AND PANTS
You will need
4m (4½yd) of 91cm (36in) wide fabric*
50cm (⅝yd) of 2cm (¾in) wide elastic
1m (1⅛yd) of narrow elastic
2m (2⅜yd) of bias binding
Metric or imperial graph paper

*Note: The pants and tunic are cut generously enough across the width to suit all sizes. After making the tunic pattern, fold up 6cm (2½in) at the wrist edge to allow for the frill turning. Now try the pattern against the child to see if it needs to be lengthened at the lower edge. If so, adjust the pattern and add four times this extra length to your fabric requirements. Check to see if the sleeve length needs adjustment also, allowing for the fact that the neck edge will be close to child's neck when gathered. The sleeves can be cut as long as desired, but this does not make any difference to the fabric requirements.

After making the pants pattern, fold up 6cm (2½in) at the ankle edge to allow for the frill turning, then try pattern against the child to see if ankle edge needs to be lengthened. If so, adjust the pattern and add twice this extra length to your fabric requirements.

To make the tunic
Copy the pattern outline onto graph paper square by square. Cut one tunic piece from fabric, having the width of fabric in the direction shown on the pattern. You will only be able to cut one tunic piece from the 91cm (36in) width. Turn over the tunic pattern and cut another piece in the same way. You now have

one pair of pieces. Join them at the centre edges to complete the front of the tunic. Cut and make the back of the tunic in the same way.

Now join tunic front to back at the shoulder edges. Turn the wrist edges 6cm (2½in) to wrong side of fabric and press. Stitch the edges of a strip of bias binding across each of the turned-in raw edges to form casings for the elastic (see diagram). Thread narrow elastic through casings to fit the child's wrists and secure elastic at each end with a few stitches.

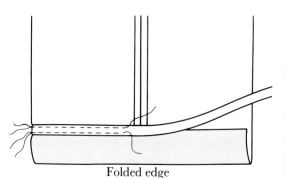

Folded edge

DIAGRAM *sewing on bias binding to form casing for the elastic*

Join tunic front to back at the under-arm edges. Stitch again at the under-arm curves to reinforce, then clip seams at curves. Hem lower edge of tunic.

Bind the neck edge of tunic with a 3cm (1¼in) wide remnant strip of the fabric, taking narrow turnings, to form a casing for the elastic and leaving a gap in the stitching. Thread narrow elastic through to fit the child's neck loosely, then join the ends.

To make the pants
Copy the pattern outline onto graph paper.

Fold the remaining piece of fabric, bringing the long selvedges together. Cut two pants pieces, placing the edge indicated on pattern to the folded edge of fabric each time. Open up the folded pieces, then turn the ankle edges 6cm (2½in) to wrong side of fabric and press. Sew on bias binding and thread through elastic in same way as for the tunic wrists, to fit the child's ankles.

Now join the pants pieces to each other at the centre edges. Stitch again at curves to reinforce seams. Clip curves in seams. Bring the centre seams together and join the inside leg edges of each leg.

Turn in the waist edge 5mm (¼in), then 2.5cm (1in) and stitch, leaving a gap in stitching. Thread the wide elastic through to fit the child's waist, join ends of elastic, then close gap in stitching.

NECK FRILL AND ROSETTES
You will need
1m (1⅛yd) of 91cm (36in) wide fabric
30cm (⅜yd) of narrow elastic
A little cotton-wool for stuffing
Fastenings for ends of frill

To make
Before cutting the strips for the frill, trim a 20cm (8in) wide strip off one selvedge of the fabric for making the rosettes.

Now cut the remaining piece of fabric in half across the width of the fabric. Join the strips at one pair of short edges. Fold the strip, bringing the long edges together. Join the long edges, then turn right side out. Press the strip, having the seam running down the centre of strip. Make a line of stitching along the strip 10cm (4in) away from one long folded edge. Stitch again, 1cm (⅜in) away from first line of stitching, thus forming casing for the elastic. Thread elastic through to fit child's neck and secure it at each end with a few stitches. Hem the remaining raw edges at ends of frill. Fold the frill at the elastic casing so that there is a double layer with one narrower than the other as can be seen in the illustration. Sew fasteners to ends of frill.

For the rosettes, cut two 20cm (8in) diameter circles from the remaining strip of fabric. Turn in the raw edges of each circle 5mm (¼in) and run round a gathering thread. Pull up gathers tightly and fasten off. Sew through gathers to centre of circle and back again. For centre of each rosette, cut an 8cm (3in) diameter circle from remnant of the other fabric. Gather round the edge of each circle, pull up gathers, stuffing circle firmly with cotton-wool. Pull gathers tightly to close and fasten off. Sew these bobbles gathered-side down to gathered centres of rosettes. Sew rosettes to centre front of tunic as illustrated.

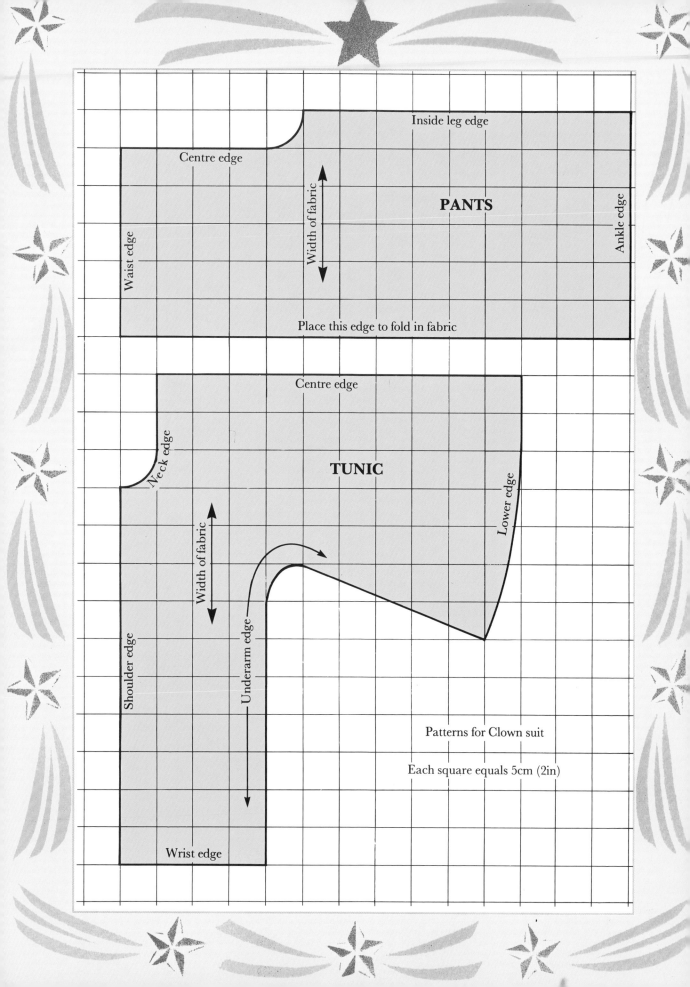

PANTS

Inside leg edge

Centre edge

Width of fabric

Waist edge

Ankle edge

Place this edge to fold in fabric

Centre edge

TUNIC

Neck edge

Width of fabric

Shoulder edge

Underarm edge

Lower edge

Wrist edge

Patterns for Clown suit

Each square equals 5cm (2in)

Count Dracula

*The count wears an elegant black semi-circular cape lined with scarlet satin.
His white satin waistcoat is very easy to make, because only the front portion
is required and it is held in place with Velcro strips and tapes tied at the back. The
'candle' is perfectly safe for children as it is constructed from a cardboard
tube and other household odds and ends.*

BASIS FOR COSTUME
Black or grey ordinary trousers
Ordinary white shirt
Black shiny shoes, or black wellingtons worn
    under the trousers
Joke fangs from a toyshop (optional)

SHIRT
Turn up the shirt collar, then fold down the
corners and press, for a wing-collar effect.

MEDALLION
You will need
50cm (1/2yd) of 2.5cm (1in) wide, purple
    ribbon
A piece of junk jewellery or brooch which
    resembles a medallion
Fastening for ends of ribbon

To make
Form the centre of ribbon length into a V-
point and sew in place. Sew the piece of
jewellery to the V-point. Turn in raw ends of
the ribbon and sew on the fastening.

BOW-TIE
You will need
A 30cm (12in) length of 4cm (1 1/2in) wide,
    white ribbon
50cm (1/2yd) of narrow white tape
Fastening for ends of tape

To make
Cut a 24cm (9 1/2in) length off the ribbon and
fold it, bringing the ends together at centre of
length. Sew ends in place. Use the remaining

piece of ribbon folded in half along the length
to wind tightly around the centre of bow. Sew
the ends together. Slot the tape through this
centre piece at back of bow and sew fastener to
ends of the tape, shortening the tape as necessary to fit around neck of shirt.

WAISTCOAT
You will need
40cm (1/2yd) of 91cm (36in) wide, white satin
    fabric*
Five small fancy buttons
A 6cm (2 1/2in) length of Velcro
70cm (3/4yd) narrow white tape
Metric or imperial graph paper

*Note: After making the waistcoat pattern, try
it against the child to see if it needs to be
lengthened. If so, adjust the length at the
shoulder edge of pattern and add this extra to
your fabric requirements. The width of the
pattern should suit all sizes.

To make
Copy the pattern outline onto graph paper
square by square.
    Bring the selvedges of fabric together. Cut
the waistcoat front pieces twice from this
double thickness of fabric, having width of
fabric in direction shown on pattern.
    Join the pairs of pieces around the edges,
leaving the shoulder edges open. Trim seams,
turn right side out and press. Turn in shoulder
edges at seam line and slip stitch. Fold back the
lapel portion, as shown by dotted line on pattern and oversew the folded back edges at the
shoulder edges to hold in place. Cut the furry
Velcro strip in half and sew one to each shoul-

der edge of the waistcoat on the wrong side.

Lay the waistcoat pieces side by side, with right sides uppermost and centre front edges together. Lap centre-front edges of waistcoat pieces 1cm (⅜in), then sew on the buttons at regular intervals, through all the thicknesses.

Cut the length of tape in two pieces and sew one end of each to the side edges of waistcoat at position shown on the pattern.

To fix waistcoat to shirt

Put the shirt, medallion and bow-tie on the child. Place waistcoat front in position, tying the tapes at the back to fit neatly.

Now place the shoulder edges of waistcoat level with the shoulder seams of the shirt. Mark the position of the Velcro strips on waistcoat, onto the shirt with pins.

Remove all items. Sew corresponding hooked strips of Velcro to the marked positions on shirt, so that shoulder edges of waistcoat can be attached to them when the waistcoat is worn.

CAPE

You will need

1.80m (2yd) of 91cm (36in) wide, black fabric
1.80m (2yd) of 91cm (36in) wide, scarlet satin fabric
10cm (⅛yd) of 82cm (32¼in) wide, firm iron-on interfacing
An 8cm (3in) length of Velcro

To make

Draw the quarter circle pattern onto a large sheet of paper to the measurements given in Diagram 1. The finished length of the cape from back neck to hem will be about 81cm (32in), which should suit most sizes. For very small children, the cape may need to be shortened, so trim off the excess at lower edge of the pattern.

Fold the black fabric in half, bringing the cut raw edges together and having selvedges level. Place one straight edge of the pattern to the fold in the fabric and cut out. Repeat this with the red fabric. Join the cape pieces around the edges, leaving the neck edges open. Trim corners of seam and clip curve at lower edge. Turn cape right side out and press. Stitch the

neck edges of cape and lining together 1cm (⅜in) away from raw edges. Clip fabric at the curve, above the stitching line.

For the collar, cut a 10 x 30cm (4 x 12in) strip of black and of red fabric from the remnants left over from the cape. Iron a strip of interfacing the same size to the wrong side of each collar strip. Join the collar pieces, leaving one pair of long edges open. Trim the seam, turn right side out and press. Turn in the long raw edges of collar 1cm (⅜in) and press. Now slip the clipped neck edge of the cape inside these edges and pin, matching the turned-in edge of collar to the stitching line on neck of cape. Tack, then stitch through all thicknesses.

To attach cape to shirt

On the inside of the cape at centre back, just below the collar, stitch a 4cm (1½in) length of furry Velcro. Sew the corresponding hooked strip to the shirt at centre back just below the collar.

Put all the costume items on the child and attach the cape to Velcro strip at back of the shirt. Mark the positions on the shirt, where the front edges of the cape (just below the collar) touch the shirt.

Sew a 2cm (¾in) length of hooked Velcro to each marked position on the shirt and the

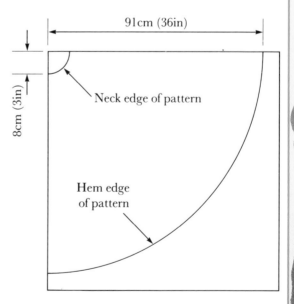

DIAGRAM 1 *drawing the cape pattern*

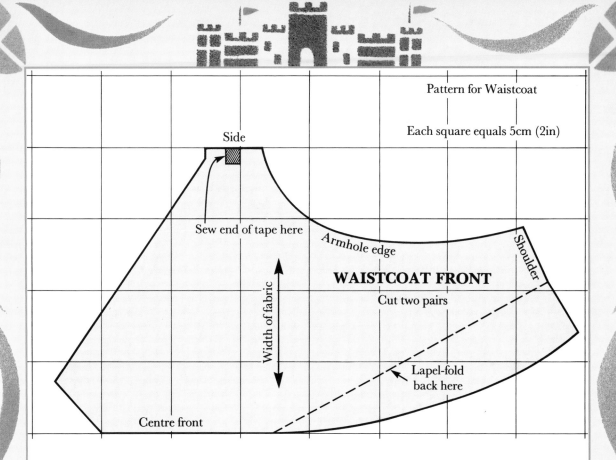

Pattern for Waistcoat

Each square equals 5cm (2in)

Side

Sew end of tape here

Armhole edge

Shoulder

WAISTCOAT FRONT

Cut two pairs

Width of fabric

Lapel-fold
back here

Centre front

corresponding furry strips to the cape fronts on the inside, just below the collar.

CANDLE

You will need

A cardboard tube from the centre of a
    paper-towel roll
White paper to cover tube
Polyfilla
White household paint
A yellow cellophane sweet wrapping-paper
Scraps of card, and red and black knitting-yarn
Adhesive

To make

Glue a strip of white paper around the cardboard tube to cover it. Stuff the tube with newspaper, then glue to one end a card circle cut to fit. Cut another circle of card the same size. Knot a short length of black yarn and pass it through the centre of the circle for the candle wick. Stiffen the wick with glue. Glue this card circle in place on the tube with the wick uppermost.

Mix up a little Polyfilla to a creamy consistency. Use a spoon to run dribbles down the candle from the top end. Allow to dry, then repeat with Polyfilla to thicken the dribbles if necessary. When quite dry, coat the candle with white paint.

Glue a little red yarn around the top of the wick, then glue a twist of cellophane around the wick for the flame.

Chorus Girl

This cute outfit is made from cotton fabric, but glittery lurex or satin material could be used for a more glamorous version. The puffed sleeves of the blouse are stiffened with interfacing and there are instructions for making the little circular hat, to complete the costume.

BASIS FOR COSTUME
A pair of tap-dancing shoes

BLOUSE, SHORTS AND HAT
You will need
1.80cm (2yd) of 91cm (36in) wide, spotted fabric
70cm (¾yd) of 91cm (36in) wide, plain fabric
70cm (¾yd) of 91cm (36in) wide, superstretch iron-on interfacing
50cm (⅝yd) of 2m (¾in) wide elastic
50cm (⅝yd) of cord elastic
Fastenings for back of blouse
Metric or imperial graph paper

Note: The blouse sleeve pattern will fit all sizes. The finished blouse when fastened measures 70cm (27½in) around the chest. It should be fairly loose on the child. If the pattern needs to be widened, add one quarter of the extra amount to the side edge of the pattern. The shoulder to hem length is 34cm (13½in), so if required, add extra to the lower edge of the pattern.

The finished shorts measure 64cm (25in) around the hip. If a larger size is required, add one quarter of the extra amount to the side edge of the pattern. The finished depth of the shorts at the side is 24cm (9½in). Lengthen the pattern if necessary, at the waist edge.

The amounts of fabric quoted are sufficient for any enlarging of the patterns, as can be seen on the cutting layout.

To make the blouse
Copy the bodice and sleeve pattern outlines onto graph paper square by square. Only one pattern for the bodice needs to be made. Simply fold in the pattern at the dotted centre-front line as shown when cutting the bodice front.

Referring to the cutting layout, cut one pair of back bodice pieces from spotted fabric. Cut one front piece, placing the folded edge of the pattern to a fold in the fabric. Join the front to back pieces at the shoulder edges.

Cut two sleeves from spotted fabric, placing edge indicated on pattern to fold in fabric each time. Cut two sleeves pieces in the same way, from the interfacing. Fuse the interfacing to the wrong side of the sleeve pieces. Run gathering threads along armhole edges of the sleeves between the dots. Sew these edges to the armhole edges of bodice, pulling up the gathers to fit and having right sides together and raw edges level. Stitch the seams again, then trim seams.

Measure around the child's arm above the elbow. Add 4cm (1½in) to this measurement. Cut two strips of the plain fabric this length by 10cm (4in) in width, for the sleeve cuffs. Gather the lower edge of each sleeve to fit one long edge of each cuff. Stitch one long edge of each cuff to the gathered edge of each sleeve, with right sides together and raw edges level. Press the seams towards the cuffs, then trim seams.

Now join bodice front to backs at the side edges and the underarm edges of sleeves and the cuff strips. Trim seams at cuffs and underarms. Turn in the raw edge of each cuff 1cm (⅜in) and slip stitch to cuff seams on the inside.

Turn in the back edges of the bodice 1cm (⅜in), then 2cm (¾in) and stitch down. Hem lower edge of the blouse.

To neaten the neck edge, cut 4cm (1½in) wide bias strips of spotted fabric, joining strips to required length. Bind the neck edge with the bias strip. Sew fasteners to back of blouse.

For the bow, cut a 20 x 25cm (8 x 10in) strip of plain fabric. Bring the 20cm (8in) edges to-

gether. Join the raw edges, leaving a gap for turning. Trim seam and corners, turn right side out and press. Slip stitch the gap.

Gather up the centre of the strip, but not too tightly. For the centre of bow, cut a 4 x 10cm (1½ x 4in) strip of plain fabric. Fold in the long edges to meet at the centre, then press. Place this strip around the gathered centre of bow, then lap and sew the ends. Sew the bow to the blouse neck at front.

To make the shorts

Referring to the cutting layout, cut two shorts pieces, placing edge of pattern to a fold each time as indicated.

For the lower edge binding, cut two 5cm (2in) wide bias strips of plain fabric the length of lower edge of shorts. Stitch one long edge of each binding strip to the lower edge of each shorts piece, having right sides together and raw edges level. Press the seams towards the bias strips, then trim seams.

Join the shorts pieces to each other at the centre edges. Stitch again at the curves to reinforce, then trim seams at curves. Bring the centre seams together, then join the inside leg edges of each leg and also short edges of bias strips. Trim the seams. Turn in the raw edges of the bias strips 1cm (⅜in) and slip stitch to seams on the wrong side.

Turn in the waist edge 1cm (⅜in), then 2.5cm (1in) and stitch down, leaving a gap for inserting the elastic. Thread elastic through to fit child's waist, then join ends. Stitch gap.

To make the sash

Cut a 10 x 91cm (4 x 36in) strip of plain fabric. Join long edges and at an angle across each short end, leaving a gap in seam for turning. Trim seam, turn right side out and press. Slip stitch gap.

To make the hat

Cut a 20 x 65cm (8 x 26in) strip of spotted fabric and of interfacing. Fuse the interfacing to wrong side of fabric strip. Join the short ends and trim seam. Turn right side out. Taking large running stitches, gather up each of the long raw edges separately. Pull up tight and fasten off. Bring both sets of gathers together at centre of hat and catch them together. Make a bow from plain fabric as given for the blouse. Sew centre of the bow to the hat gathers, so that bow stands upright on the hat.

Cut a 15 x 20cm (6 x 8in) strip of spotted fabric. Fold with right side outside, bringing the 20cm (8in) edges together. Gather all round the raw edges through both thicknesses. Pull gathers up tight and fasten off. Sew the gathered portion to hat just behind the bow to hold bow upright. Catch this piece to the bow.

Sew ends of the cord elastic under centre of the hat, trimming length to suit the child's head.

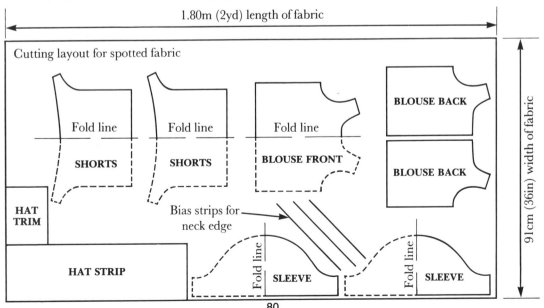

1.80m (2yd) length of fabric

Cutting layout for spotted fabric

BLOUSE BACK

Fold line   Fold line   Fold line

SHORTS   SHORTS   BLOUSE FRONT   BLOUSE BACK

HAT TRIM

Bias strips for neck edge

HAT STRIP   Fold line   SLEEVE   Fold line   SLEEVE

91cm (36in) width of fabric

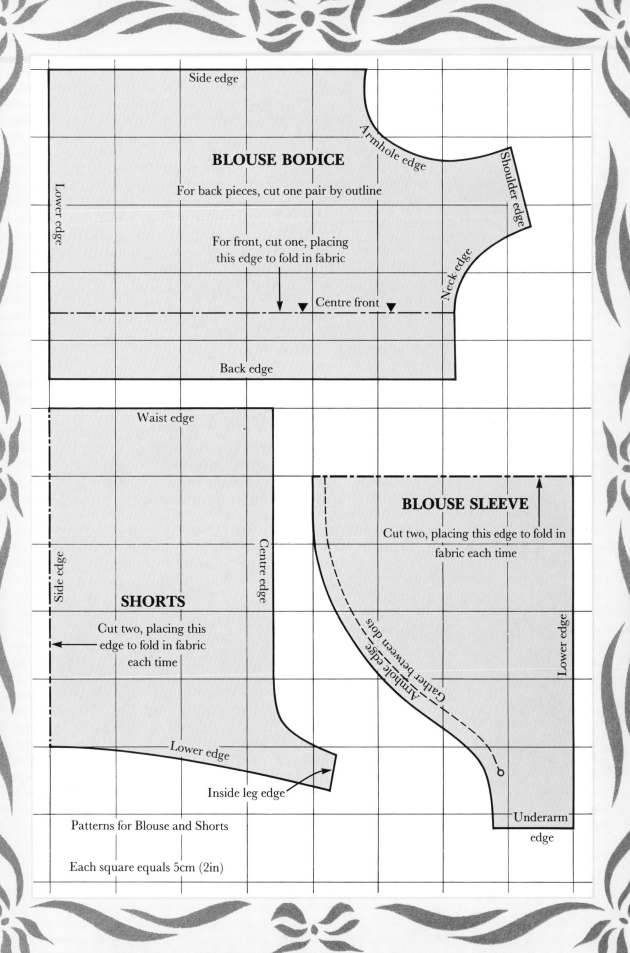

BLOUSE BODICE

For back pieces, cut one pair by outline

For front, cut one, placing this edge to fold in fabric

Side edge

Armhole edge

Shoulder edge

Lower edge

Neck edge

Centre front

Back edge

Waist edge

BLOUSE SLEEVE

Cut two, placing this edge to fold in fabric each time

Side edge

Centre edge

SHORTS

Cut two, placing this edge to fold in fabric each time

Lower edge

Armhole edge

Gather between dots

Lower edge

Inside leg edge

Underarm edge

Patterns for Blouse and Shorts

Each square equals 5cm (2in)

Movie Star

You can make this glamorous outfit from the most glittery of fabrics, or use shiny dress-lining material as an inexpensive alternative. The sparkly silver trimming is tinsel garland as used for decorating the tree at Christmas. No special patterns are required for the costume, just straight strips of fabric.

DRESS AND HEAD-DRESS

You will need

1.60cm (1¾yd) of 91cm (36in) wide fabric for the dress*

Silver Christmas tree tinsel garland – a total length of 5m (5½yd)

1m (1⅛yd) of 91cm (36in) wide net fabric for the lining frill inside the hem frill*

An oddment of contrast fabric for the belt and head-dress decoration

Short length of narrow elastic for head-dress

Fastenings for the dress and the belt

*Note: From the measurements given in the instructions, the finished waist to hem skirt-length will be about 60cm (23½in). If a shorter or longer skirt is required, the adjustment can be made on the hem frill. This frill is 25cm (10in) deep and two of these pieces are required, cut across the complete 91cm (36in) width of the fabric (see cutting layout). For a longer skirt, you will therefore need to add *twice* the extra length needed to the dress fabric and the net fabric requirements.

Since all the pieces needed are straight strips, refer to the cutting layout for the most economical way of cutting the pieces.

DIAGRAM 1 *showing measurements for the bodice fabric strips*

To make the bodice

Cut two strips of fabric to the measurements given in Diagram 1. As a general guide, for a child of 100-110cm (3ft 3in-3ft 7in) in height, the *width* of each strip should be about 16cm (6¼in) which includes seam allowances.

Join the bodice pieces around the edges, leaving one pair of long edges open. Trim corners of seam. Turn right side out and press. The remaining raw edges will be the waist edges of the bodice.

For the shoulder straps, cut two 8 x 34cm (3 x 13½in) strips of fabric. Join long edges and across one short end of each strip. Trim seams and corners. Turn straps right side out and press.

Put the bodice around the child, then overlap and pin the short edges at centre back as necessary to fit the chest neatly. Pin the ends of the shoulder straps to the bodice at front and back, adjusting lengths of straps as necessary, so that top edge of bodice fits just under the arms as shown in Diagram 2, page 20.

Remove the bodice and adjust strap positions if necessary, so that they are exactly the same distance apart and equal in length. Stitch along top edge of bodice and through the straps. Trim any excessive length off the straps, then sew the ends in place. Note that the ends of the straps will be on the inside

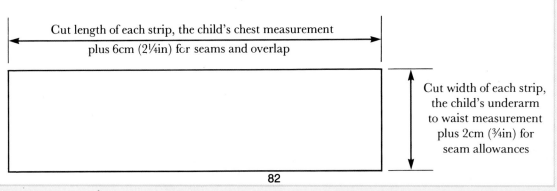

Cut length of each strip, the child's chest measurement plus 6cm (2¼in) for seams and overlap

Cut width of each strip, the child's underarm to waist measurement plus 2cm (¾in) for seam allowances

(wrong side) of the bodice when making up the rest of the dress.

To make the skirt

Cut two 40 x 45cm (16 x 18in) pieces of fabric as shown on the cutting layout. Join them at one 40cm (16in) edge, taking a 2cm (¾in) seam and leaving a 16cm (6¼in) gap at one end of the seam for the back waist opening. Press seam to one side and neaten raw edges of the opening.

Join the remaining 40cm (16in) edges from the waist edges downwards, leaving 24cm (9½in) open at lower end of seam for the centre front opening of the skirt.

For the hem frill, cut two 25 x 91cm (10 x 36in) strips of fabric. Remember to make adjustment to the 25cm (10in) measurement if a shorter or longer skirt is required. Join the frill strips at one pair of short edges. Gather one long edge to fit around the lower edge of the skirt. Stitch frill in place with right sides of fabric together and raw edges level.

Trim off the lower corners of the frill at centre front, forming a wide curve. Now turn in all the raw edges of frill and of centre front opening of the skirt 1cm (⅜in) and stitch in place.

For the inner net frill, cut the net in half across the width of the fabric, then join the two strips at one pair of short edges. Fold the entire strip in half, bringing the long edges together. Gather along the folded edge to fit the lower edge of the dress *skirt* (not the hem frill). Sew this gathered edge to the gathered edge of the skirt frill on the inside of the dress. Trim lower corners of the net frill in a curve to match the skirt frill.

Gather the waist edge of the dress skirt to fit lower edge of the bodice. Pin in place, having right sides together, raw edges level and leaving the bodice lining free. Make sure at this stage that you have pinned the right side of the *bodice* to the skirt and not the *lining*. Stitch skirt to bodice as pinned. Turn in the waist edge of bodice lining at seam line and slip stitch it over the seam. Sew fastenings to back edges of bodice and skirt opening.

Hand sew the tinsel garland around the hem edge of the skirt frill and up the centre front edges as far as the waist seam, as follows. Hav-

ing wrong side of fabric towards you, hold the tinsel against the right side of the fabric, then take large oversewing stitches through fabric and into the centre cord of the tinsel. Sew a continuous length of tinsel over shoulder straps and across neck of bodice at front and back in the same way as for the skirt.

To make the belt

Cut a 14cm (5½in) wide strip of contrast fabric, the child's waist measurement, plus 6cm (2¼in). Join long edges and across one short end of the strip. Turn right side out. Turn in the remaining raw edge and slip stitch. Gather the belt up tightly at centre and sew to waist edge of the bodice at centre front. Sew fastenings to short ends of belt to overlap the ends at the back of the dress as necessary, when the dress is worn.

To make the head-dress

Measure around the child's head and cut a strip of the dress fabric this size by 14cm (5½in). Make as for the belt and gather the strip at centre. Gather up each end tightly also. Sew a short length of elastic to these gathered ends so that the head-dress fits the child's head comfortably. Make a few gathered-up rosettes of the dress fabric and the contrast fabric and sew to one side of the head-dress, together with oddments of tinsel.

FUR STOLE

You will need
25cm (10in) of 138cm (54in) wide white fur fabric

To make

Join the long edges of the fur fabric strip and across short ends, rounding off the corners and leaving a gap in one long edge for turning. Trim the corners, turn right side out and slip stitch the gap.

JEWELLERY

Use any suitable necklace and bracelet. Alternatively, sew Velcro strips to the ends of lengths of lurex and sequin braid, adding a small pendant to the necklace braid as shown in the illustration.

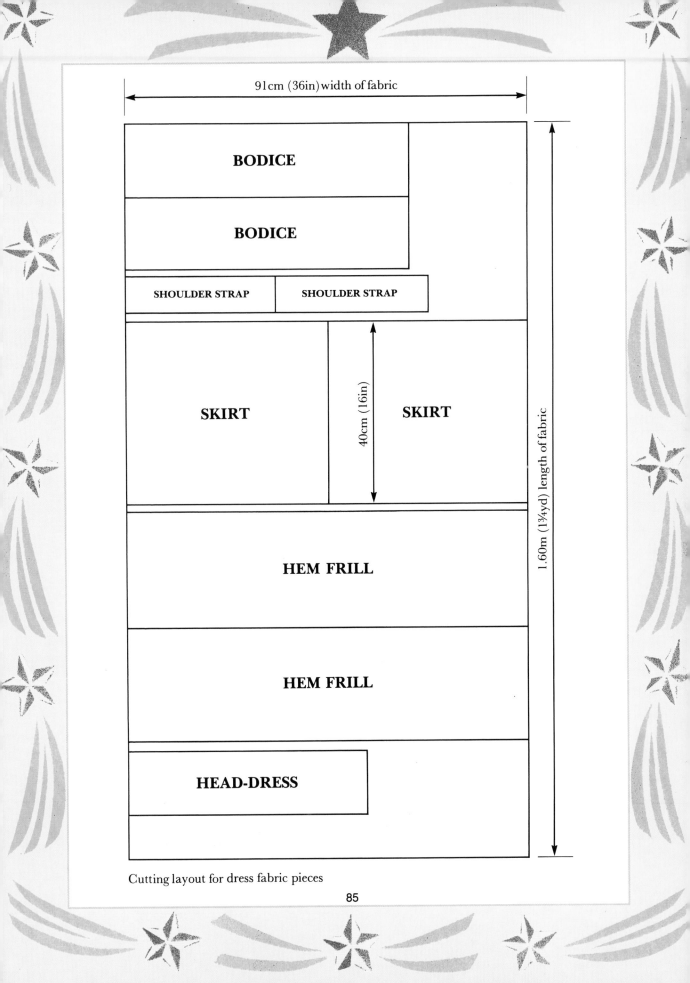

91 cm (36 in) width of fabric

BODICE

BODICE

SHOULDER STRAP   SHOULDER STRAP

SKIRT

40 cm (16 in)

SKIRT

HEM FRILL

HEM FRILL

HEAD-DRESS

1.60 m (1¾ yd) length of fabric

Cutting layout for dress fabric pieces

Latin Lover

Wellington boots and a plain white shirt form the basis for this dashing
Valentino-style outfit. The poncho can be worn in the usual way, but it looks
best folded and thrown casually over one shoulder as shown in the illustration.
For the pants, choose a fabric which does not fray and drapes well,
such as polyester jersey.

BASIS FOR COSTUME
Black wellington boots
Ordinary white shirt
A hat with flat crown and brim, from a toyshop
A long scarf for the waist sash

NECKTIE AND HATBAND
You will need
1m (1⅛yd) of thick fancy cord
1.20m (1⅜yd) of plain dressing-gown cord

To make
Tie knots near to the ends of the cords, then
fray out ends. Tie the fancy cord under shirt
collar and in a bow at the front. Knot the plain
cord around the hat so that the ends hang
down to one side.

PANTS
You will need
80cm (⅞yd) of 138cm (54in) wide polyester
 jersey fabric*
40cm (½yd) of 2m (¾in) wide elastic
Fastenings for waistband and back opening of
 pants
Metric or imperial graph paper

*Note: The pants are cut wide enough to fit any
hip size. After making the pattern, check the
leg length against the child. The ankle edge
should be level with child's ankles. Shorten or
lengthen the ankle edge of pattern to suit. If
you need to lengthen the pattern, add this
extra length to your fabric requirements.

To make
Copy the pattern outline onto graph paper,
square by square. From one end of the fabric,
cut a 10cm (4in) wide strip across the full
width of the fabric and lay it aside to use for the
waistband.

Fold the selvedges of the remaining fabric in,
so that they meet at the centre of the width of
the fabric. Cut two pants pieces, placing edge
of pattern indicated to one of the folds each
time. Join the two pants pieces to each other at
the centre edges, leaving 16cm (6¼in) open
at waist end of one seam for centre-back
opening. Stitch again at curves in seams to
reinforce, then clip curves in seams. Neaten
the raw edges of the centre-back opening, then
press seam to one side.

Bring the centre seams together and join the
inside leg edges of each leg. Turn the ankle
edges 2.5cm (1in) to wrong side and stitch
down, leaving a gap in stitching for threading
through the elastic. Thread elastic through
casings and join ends to fit child's legs loosely
above the tops of the boots. This is done in
order to create the blousey fullness which
hangs down over the boot tops. The pants are
not meant to be tucked inside the boots. Close
gaps in stitching.

Gather the waist edge of the pants to fit the
child's waist, allowing a little extra for an overlap. Bind the gathered edge with a piece of the
10cm (4in) wide strip of fabric cut to length.
Sew fasteners to the ends of the waistband and
to open back edges of the pants. Tie the sash
around the waist as shown when the pants are
worn.

PONCHO
You will need
90cm (1yd) of 91cm (36in) wide striped fabric
3.60m (4yd) of fringe trimming

To make

Cut a slash for the neck opening across the width at the centre of the fabric, making it large enough to slip over the child's head. Neaten the raw edges of slash. Hem all the outer edges of poncho, then sew fringe to all the hemmed edges.

WHIP

You will need

A cardboard tube from the centre of a paper-towel roll

Oddments of brown felt, glittery braid, chunky brown knitting-yarn and sticky tape

A 36cm (14in) length of cord for the handle loop

Adhesive

To make

For the handle, cut once along the full length of the cardboard tube. Lap the cut edges of the tube, to make a tapered shape as shown in the illustration. Hold the cut edge in place with bits of sticky tape. Trim the card level at the widest end of the handle. Cut six 1m (1yd) lengths of chunky yarn, then secure them around the narrow end of the handle with sticky tape. Plait the yarn strands, very loosely at first, then more and more tightly towards the ends. Knot sewing thread around the ends to secure plait.

Cover the whip handle by gluing around a piece of felt cut to fit. Decorate the handle by gluing strips of braid around it as shown in the illustration.

Make a hole right through the handle, about 2.5cm (1in) down from the widest end, then thread the length of cord through and knot the ends together. Finally, cut a circle of card to fit the widest (open) end of handle, glue on felt to cover the card, then glue the circle in place.

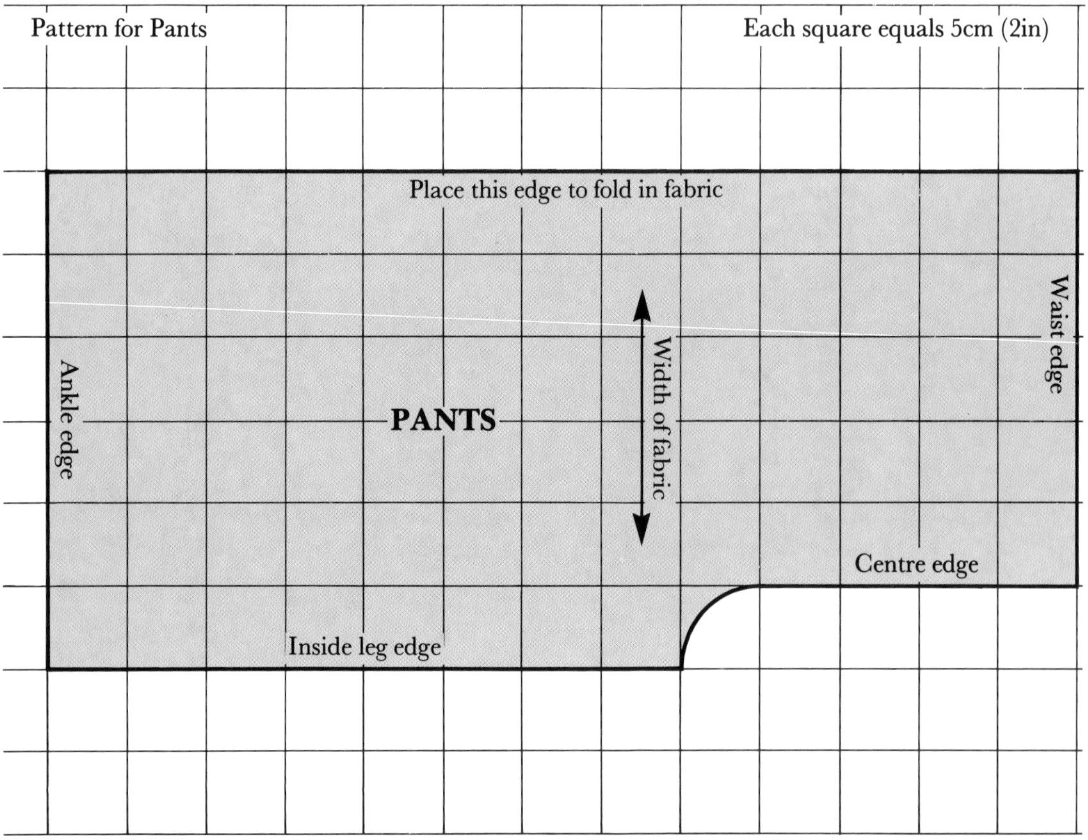

Pattern for Pants — Each square equals 5cm (2in)

Place this edge to fold in fabric

Ankle edge

PANTS

Width of fabric

Waist edge

Centre edge

Inside leg edge

Cavalier

The jacket, pants and cape of this flamboyant outfit are all made from ribbed curtain material which has a slight sheen. Fancy braid, stitched to the edges, adds extra touches of colour. All the garments are very easy to make and the jacket has only two seams since it is made from a one-piece T-shaped pattern. There are instructions for making the felt hat, but alternatively you could buy a hat from a toyshop.

BASIS FOR COSTUME
Ordinary white shirt
Black wellington boots
A rapier from a toyshop

JACKET, PANTS AND CAPE
You will need
2.50cm (2¾yd) of 122cm (48in) wide plain curtain fabric*
50cm (⅝yd) of 2cm (¾in) wide elastic
1m (1⅛yd) of narrow elastic
7.30m (8yd) of fancy braid, about 2.5m (1in) wide
1.50m (1¾yd) of 7cm (2¾in) wide white lace edging
A 10cm (4in) length of Velcro
Metric or imperial graph paper

*Note: The finished jacket measures 33cm (13¼in) from neck to lower edge. It should be below waist length on the child as shown in the illustration. If the jacket pattern needs to be lengthened at lower edge, add *twice* the extra length to fabric requirements.

The measurement around the finished jacket is 74cm (29in), but this size can be adjusted by adding extra to the side edges of the pattern and no extra fabric is needed as can be seen on the cutting layout. In the same way, the wrist edges can be lengthened also.

After making the pants pattern, try it against the child wearing the boots. Adjust the lower edge so that it is about 5cm (2in) below the level of the boot tops. If you should need to add any extra to the length of this pattern, add this amount to fabric requirements. The pants measure 72cm (28½in) around the hips, and for larger sizes, add *one quarter* of the extra amount required to the long straight edge of the pattern. You can do this without buying extra fabric as can be seen on the cutting layout (see pp92-3).

To make the jacket
Copy the pattern outline onto graph paper square by square. Referring to the cutting layout, cut the jacket from folded fabric as shown, placing the shoulder edge of the pattern to the fold. Cut the jacket open at centre front as shown on the layout.

Join the front to back at the continuous underarm and side edges. Reinforce stitching at curves, then clip seams here. Turn the centre front and lower edges 1cm (⅜in) to *right* side of fabric and stitch down. Stitch on braid to cover these raw edges, mitring it at lower corners of the jacket.

Hem each wrist edge to form casing for the elastic, leaving a small gap in stitching. Thread narrow elastic through each casing and join ends to fit child's wrists loosely. Close gaps in stitching.

To bind the neck edge, cut a 6 x 45cm (2½ x 18in) strip of fabric (see layout) and use this to bind the raw neck edge of the jacket to neaten it.

Cut a 5cm (2in) strip of hooked and of furry Velcro. Sew one end of the hooked strip just inside neck edge of jacket with hooks facing outwards. Sew furry strip to the inside of opposite neck edge of jacket.

To make the pants
Copy the pattern outline onto graph paper. Referring to the cutting layout, cut two pants pieces as shown, placing the long straight edge of pattern to fold in fabric each time. After cutting, press the folded edges to make crease lines. Stitch braid down each of the crease lines.

Hem lower edges of pants legs. Cut the length of lace edging in half. Gather each strip of lace at one long edge to fit lower edge of each pants piece. Stitch in place through the gathers, along the hemmed stitching lines. Thread narrow elastic through each hem to fit child's leg loosely. Secure elastic at ends of casings with a few stitches.

Now join the pants pieces to each other at centre edges. Reinforce stitching at the curves, then trim seams at curves. Bring these centre seams together, then join inside leg edges of each leg and also the ends of the lace frills.

Turn in the waist edge 5mm (¼in), then 2.5cm (1in) and stitch down, leaving a gap in the stitching. Thread the wide elastic through to fit the child's waist and join the ends. Close gap in the stitching.

To make the cape
The cape is a complete circle of fabric. Draw a quarter circle pattern onto a large sheet of paper as shown in the diagram.

Fold the remaining piece of fabric into quarters as shown on the cutting layout, then cut out the cape. Cut the cape open once from hem to neck edge, for the centre front edges.

Turn all the raw edges of cape 1cm (⅜in) to the *right* side and stitch down, clipping the neck edge within the 1cm (⅜in) so that it will turn easily. Stitch on braid all round the edges of the cape to cover the raw edges, easing braid around the curves and mitring at the corners.

Sew one end of a 14cm (5½in) length of braid to the inside of one neck edge at centre front. Neaten other end of braid, then sew one end of remaining hooked Velcro strip to it, having hooks facing outwards. Sew the furry Velcro strip to inside of other neck edge of cape. When worn, the neck edge of the cape should be under the lace collar.

COLLAR AND CUFFS
You will need
50cm (⅝yd) of 91cm (36in) wide white cotton fabric
2m (2¼yd) of 7cm (2¾in) wide white lace edging
40cm (16in) length of thin cord for collar ties
A 5cm (2in) length of Velcro

Metric or imperial graph paper

To make the collar
Cut a 12 x 64cm (4¾ x 25in) strip of fabric. Narrowly hem the raw edges except for one long edge. Sew lace edging to the strip so that the fancy edge of the lace extends just beyond the long hemmed edge of the collar. Gather the long raw edge to fit around the folded edge of the child's ordinary shirt collar. Bind the gathered edge with a 4cm (1½in) wide straight strip of the white fabric. Cut the cord in half and sew one end of each length to the ends of the collar binding. Tack the binding to the fold in the shirt collar so that it can be removed as required. Tie lace collar cords at the front when worn.

To make the cuffs
Copy the pattern outline from the pattern onto graph paper. Cut four cuff pieces, placing the edge of the pattern indicated to fold in fabric each time. Tack the cuffs together in pairs. Turn in the wrist and upper edges 1cm (⅜in), clipping at the curves, then stitch down.

Now stitch lace edging, slightly gathered to the wrist edge of each cuff, having gathered edge of lace and wrist edge of cuff level. Stitch another slightly gathered strip of lace to cuff further up the cuff so that the fabric is completely covered.

Join the side edges of each cuff, leaving 6cm (2¼in) open at wrist ends of seams. Turn in and stitch down these open edges. Cut the Velcro into 2.5cm (1in) lengths. Sew to open wrist edges of cuffs in the same way as for the cape fastening.

HAT
You will need
60cm (¾yd) of 91cm (36in) wide felt
50cm (⅝yd) of 82cm (32¼in) wide heavy sew-in interfacing
A few large feathers or lengths of marabou trimming
1.30m (1½yd) of bias binding to match the felt
Adhesive
Metric or imperial graph paper

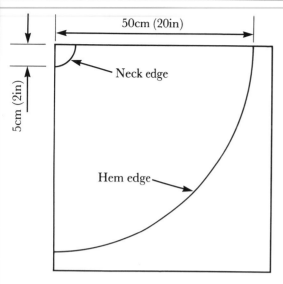

50cm (20in)

5cm (2in)

Neck edge

Hem edge

DIAGRAM *drawing the cape pattern*

To make

For the hat brim, cut a 40cm (16in) diameter circle of interfacing. Cut a 17cm (6¾in) diameter circle from the centre and discard it. This hole will fit a head measurement of up to 53cm (21in). Try the brim on the child to see if the centre hole requires enlarging.

Spread a little adhesive near to the outer and inner edges of the brim and place it on the felt near to one corner. Cut out the felt level with the outer and inner edges of the brim.

Now glue the other interfacing side of the brim to felt in the same way and cut out as be-

fore. Bind the outer edge of the brim with bias binding. Machine zig-zag around the inner hole, or stitch round close to the edges.

Copy the hat side-piece pattern outline onto graph paper. If you made the inner circle of the hat brim larger, this pattern will have to be lengthened at the centre-back edge. You can try this out by cutting the shape from folded paper to get the full-sized pattern. After adjusting if necessary, cut the hat side-piece from folded interfacing, placing the pattern to the fold as indicated. Open up the piece and stick one side only to a piece of felt. Cut out the felt level with the interfacing. Zig-zag or stitch close to the edges. Join the centre-back edges, taking a tiny seam. Turn right side out.

Place the lower edge of the hat side onto the centre hole of the brim. Oversew the edges together closely on the inside.

For the hat crown, a circle is required to fit the top of the hat. If you have not altered the pattern, the circle will be 11.5cm (4½in) in diameter. If pattern has been altered, you will have to try out larger circles to find the correct size.

Cut the circle from interfacing, glue it on to felt, cut out and finish the edges as for the side piece. Turn the hat wrong side out, then oversew edge of circle to the top. Turn right side out and sew on the feathers.

Turn the hat brim up at one side and catch the brim to the hat side.

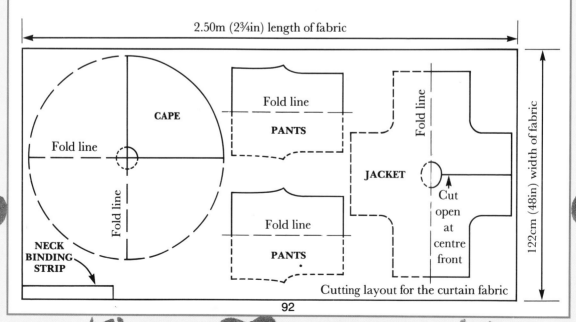

2.50m (2¾in) length of fabric

CAPE

Fold line

Fold line

PANTS

Fold line

Fold line

PANTS

Fold line

JACKET

Cut open at centre front

NECK BINDING STRIP

122cm (48in) width of fabric

Cutting layout for the curtain fabric

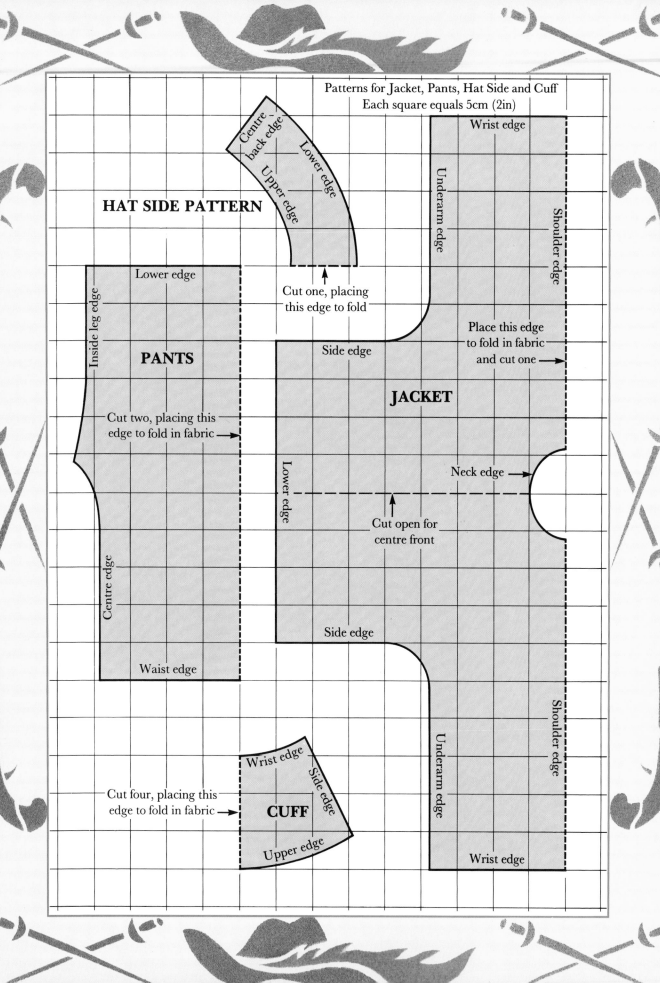

Patterns for Jacket, Pants, Hat Side and Cuff
Each square equals 5cm (2in)

HAT SIDE PATTERN

Centre back edge
Lower edge
Upper edge

Cut one, placing
this edge to fold

Wrist edge
Underarm edge
Shoulder edge

PANTS

Inside leg edge
Lower edge

Cut two, placing this
edge to fold in fabric →

Centre edge

Waist edge

Side edge

JACKET

Place this edge
to fold in fabric
and cut one →

Lower edge

Neck edge →

Cut open for
centre front

Side edge

Underarm edge

Shoulder edge

CUFF

Cut four, placing this
edge to fold in fabric →

Wrist edge
Side edge
Upper edge

Wrist edge

Pop Star

This colourful outfit is made from yellow non-woven curtain fabric, with glittery blue lamé and gold braid trimmings. The 'microphone' is made from a marker pen and a table-tennis ball.

JACKET, BELT AND PANTS

You will need

1.80cm (2yd) of 122cm (48in) wide non-woven or other firm fabric*
90cm (1yd) of 91cm (36in) wide contrast colour lamé fabric
2.20m (2½yd) of 4cm (1½in) wide fancy lurex braid
1.90m (2⅛yd) of 2cm (¾in) wide lurex braid
50cm (⅝yd) of 2cm (¾in) wide elastic
A large buckle
2 large snap-fasteners
Metric or imperial graph paper

*Note: The jacket measures 37cm (14¾in) from neck to lower edge and should be about hip length. If the jacket pattern needs to be lengthened, do this at lower edge, then add *twice* the extra length to fabric requirements.

The measurement around the finished jacket is 74cm (29in), but this size can be adjusted by adding extra to the side edges of the pattern and no extra fabric is needed, as can be seen on the cutting layout. In the same way, the wrist edges can be lengthened also.

After making the pants pattern, try it against the child to see if lower edge needs to be shortened or lengthened. If you add extra to the pattern, add this amount to fabric requirements. The pants measure 72cm (28½in) around the hips, and for larger sizes, add one quarter of the extra amount required to the long straight edge of the pattern. You can do this without buying extra fabric as can be seen on the cutting layout. The amount of lamé fabric is sufficient for all sizes.

To make the jacket

Copy the pattern outline onto graph paper square by square. Referring to the cutting layout, cut the jacket from folded yellow fabric as shown, placing the shoulder edge of the pattern to the fold. After cutting out, press the folded edge at shoulders to make a crease. Cut the jacket open at centre front as shown on the layout. Sew narrow braid to each shoulder crease, starting at the neck edge and stopping short 10cm (4in) away from the wrist edges.

Now cut a 16cm (6½in) wide strip of lamé fabric to fit right across each jacket sleeve at the wrist edge, as shown by the shaded portion on the jacket pattern. Turn in one long edge of each strip 1cm (⅜in) and stitch down. Place in position on the sleeves with the long raw edges of lamé level with wrist edges of sleeves. Sew in place all around the edges. Stitch a strip of the wide lurex braid to each lamé piece on each sleeve at the position shown in the illustration.

Now join jacket front to back at the continuous underarm and side edges. Reinforce stitching at curves, then clip seams here. Turn in centre front and lower edges 1cm (⅜in) and stitch down. Take narrow hems on the wrist edges. Sew a snap-fastener to the edges of jacket fronts at the position of child's waist.

For the collar, cut two 8 x 42cm (3 x 16½in) strips of yellow fabric and one of lamé. Place lamé right side up on top of one collar strip right side up and tack them together around the edges. Stitch a strip of the wide braid across this collar piece on top of the lamé. Join this collar piece to the other collar piece around the edges right sides together, leaving one pair of long edges open. Trim seam and corners, turn right side out and press.

Clip curved neck edge of the jacket within the 1cm (⅜in) seam allowance. Pin the right side of the long raw edge of the untrimmed collar strip to the right side neck edge of the jacket, having the raw edges of both level. Stitch in place. Turn in the remaining long raw edge of collar at seam line and slip stitch it over the seam.

To make the belt

If the buckle has a centre prong, remove it. Cut a 20 x 80cm (8 x 32in) strip of lamé fabric. Fold it, bringing the long edges together with the wrong side outside. Trim at an angle at one short end. Join the raw edges of the belt, leaving the straight short edges open. Trim corners of seam. Turn belt right side out and press. Turn in and slip stitch remaining raw edge, then sew this end around the centre bar of the buckle, gathering fabric to fit.

Fasten the belt around the child's waist on top of the jacket and mark the position where the belt fabric has passed through the buckle, so that snap-fastener halves can be sewn on to prevent the belt slipping. Sew on the snap-fastener.

To make the pants

Copy the pattern outline onto graph paper. Referring to the cutting layout, cut two pants pieces from yellow fabric as shown, placing the long straight edge of the pattern to a fold in the fabric each time. After cutting, press the folded edges to make crease lines. Stitch narrow braid down each crease line, starting at the waist edge and stopping short 10cm (4in) away from the ankle edges.

Now cut a 16cm (6½in) wide strip of lamé fabric to fit right across each pants piece at the ankle edge, as shown by the shaded portion on the pants pattern. Sew on these pieces and add braid as for the jacket sleeves.

Join the pants pieces to each other at the centre edges. Reinforce stitching at the curves, then trim seams at curves. Bring these centre seams together, then join inside leg edges of each leg.

Turn in the waist edge 5mm (¼in), then 2.5cm (1in) and stitch down, leaving a gap in the stitching. Thread elastic through to fit the child's waist, then join the ends. Close gap in stitching. Narrowly hem ankle edges.

MICROPHONE

A chunky marker pen (without ink)
A table-tennis ball
Oddment of glittery or plain stretchy fabric, such as a cutting from tights or stocking
Thin cord, for the microphone lead
Short length of braid
Adhesive

To make

If the pen is made of plastic, you will be able to rub off the lettering with a scouring pad. If it is made of metal, then glue round a strip of coloured paper to cover the lettering.

Remove the lid. Pierce a hole in the lid-top, then thread one end of the cord through and knot it on the inside of the lid. Replace the lid on the pen, gluing in place if necessary.

Glue the table-tennis ball to the other end of the pen. Place a piece of stretchy fabric over the ball and pull it tightly down onto the pen, gathering up to enclose the ball. Wind sewing thread tightly around the gathers, just below the ball and knot ends. Trim off excess fabric close to the gathers. Glue a strip of braid around the pen to cover gathered raw edges.

JEWELLERY

Add chunky junk jewellery, such as a thick gold neck chain with medallion, and a gold bracelet.

PANTS — Fold line

PANTS — Fold line

1.80m (2yd) length of fabric

COLLAR STRIP

JACKET

COLLAR STRIP

Fold line

Cut open at centre front →

122cm (48in) width of fabric

Cutting layout for the yellow fabric

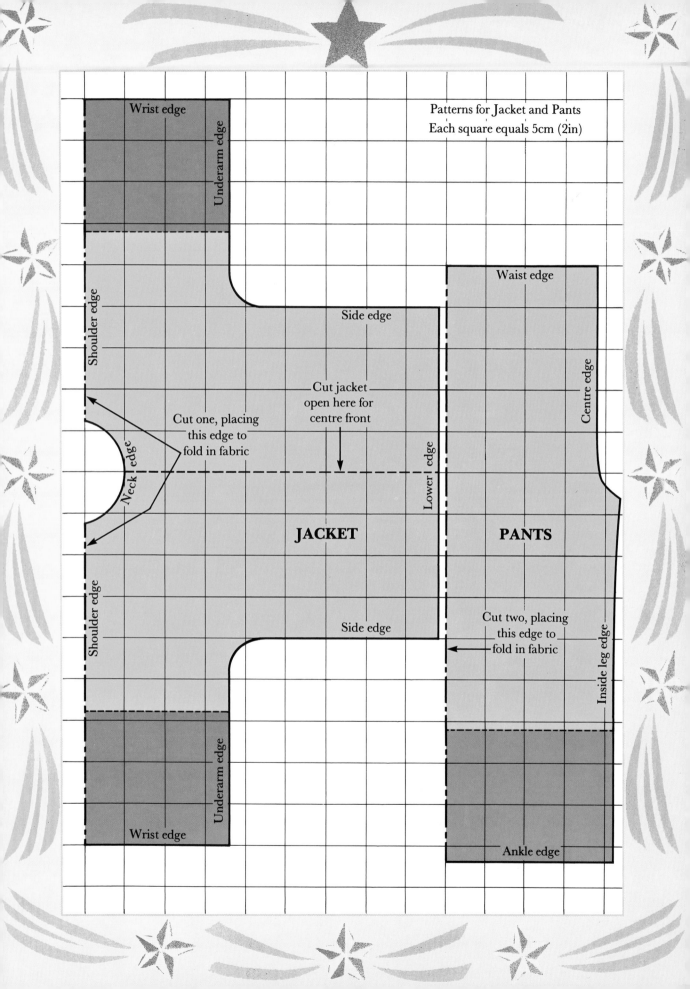

Patterns for Jacket and Pants
Each square equals 5cm (2in)

JACKET

PANTS

Wrist edge

Underarm edge

Shoulder edge

Neck edge

Cut one, placing
this edge to
fold in fabric

Side edge

Cut jacket
open here for
centre front

Lower edge

Shoulder edge

Side edge

Underarm edge

Wrist edge

Waist edge

Centre edge

Cut two, placing
this edge to
fold in fabric

Inside leg edge

Ankle edge

Victorian Miss

This charming taffeta dress is made entirely from straight strips of fabric. The tartan checks make easy work of cutting straight edges – you only need to measure once for each strip, then follow the woven lines of the checks. A petticoat gives fullness to the dress skirt, but a crinoline underskirt could be made instead, as given for Miss Charlotte's costume on p48.

DRESS

You will need

5.50m (6yd) of 91cm (36in) wide tartan taffeta fabric

2.80m (3⅛yd) of narrow white lace edging

A 30cm (12in) square of white lace fabric

40cm (½yd) of narrow elastic

1.30m (1½yd) of 5cm (2in) wide ribbon to match the dress

Fastenings for dress bodice and skirt opening

Note: If you decide on a crinoline underskirt, make this first so that the dress can be tried on *over* the crinoline to find the required skirt length.

The skirt length is adjustable on this dress, according to where the frill is attached. If the gathered edge of the frill is sewn to the hemmed edge of the skirt, this gives a maximum skirt length of 80cm (32½in) from waist to hem of frill.

When cutting strips of fabric which have to be joined to other strips (for example the hem frill pieces), make sure that the checks will match at the joined edges. Extra fabric has been allowed for matching the checks.

When cutting out all the strips of fabric, al-ways have the *longest* measurement given for each strip, going *across* the 91cm (36in) *width* of the fabric.

The skirt

Cut three 64cm (25in) wide pieces by the 91cm (36in) width of the fabric. Join them to each other at the selvedges, leaving 16cm (6¼in) open at the end of one seam for the centre-back opening of the skirt. Press this seam to one side. Narrowly hem the lower raw edge of the skirt.

For the skirt frill, cut six 25cm (10in) wide pieces by the 91cm (36in) width of the fabric. Join them to each other at the selvedges to form a continuous length, then narrowly hem one long edge. Turn in the remaining long raw edge 2cm (¾in) and press. Gather the frill 1cm (⅜in) away from the folded edge to fit around the skirt. Lay the skirt and frill aside until required.

The bodice

Cut two strips of fabric (one for the bodice and one for the lining) to the measurements given in Diagram 1. As a general guide, for a child of 100-110cm (3ft 3in-3ft 7in) the *width* of each

---

Cut length of each strip, the child's chest measurement

plus 6cm (2¼in) for seams and overlap

Cut width of each strip, the child's underarm to waist measurement plus 2cm (¾in) for seam allowances

DIAGRAM 1 *measurements for the bodice fabric strips*

strip should be about 16cm (6¼in) which includes seam allowances. Join the pieces around the edges, leaving one pair of long edges open. Trim corners of seam, turn right side out and press. Tack the long raw edges together for waist edge of bodice.

For the shoulder straps, cut two 8 x 34cm (3 x 13½in) strips of fabric. Join the long edges and across one short end of each strip. Trim seams and corners. Turn straps right side out and press.

Put the bodice around the child, then overlap and pin the short edges at centre back as necessary, to fit the chest neatly. Pin the ends of the shoulder straps to the bodice at the front and back, adjusting the length of straps as necessary, so that the top edge of the bodice fits just under the arms as shown in Diagram 2.

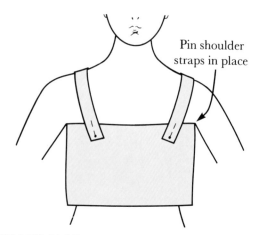

Pin shoulder straps in place

DIAGRAM 2

Remove the bodice and adjust strap positions if necessary, so that they are exactly the same distance apart and equal in length. Stitch along the top edge of the bodice and through the straps. Trim any excessive length off the straps, then sew the ends in place.

Note that the ends of the straps will be on the inside (wrong side) of the bodice when making up the rest of the dress.

The sleeves

Cut two 22 x 58cm (8½ x 23in) strips of fabric. Join the short edges of each sleeve strip. Turn in one long edge of each sleeve 5mm (¼in), then 8cm (3in) and press. Stitch the folded-in edges in place, leaving a gap in stitching for inserting the elastic. Stitch again, 1cm (⅜in) away from the first stitching line, through the double thickness of fabric, to complete the casing for the elastic.

Sew lace edging to the pressed folded edge of each sleeve. Thread elastic through the casings to fit the child's upper arms. Join ends of elastic and close gaps in the casings.

Now gather the remaining long raw edges of each sleeve, pulling up the gathers to fit the armhole edges of bodice – that is, along the outer edge of each shoulder strap and underarm edge of bodice between the ends of each strap. Space out the gathers evenly. Having the right sides of sleeves and bodice outside, tack the gathered raw edges of sleeves in position, just inside the edges of straps and bodice. Top stitch in place along the straps and bodice.

To assemble the skirt and bodice

Gather the waist edge of the skirt to fit the waist edge of the bodice. Stitch in place, having the right sides together and raw edges level. Fold the waist seam up against the bodice, then top stitch around the bodice, just above the waist seam, to hold seam in place.

To attach the frill

Put the dress on the child (with crinoline underneath if you have made one), then lap and pin the bodice edges at the back. Check the skirt length. It should be *above* ground level, but on a very small child the skirt may need to be shortened. If so, trim off excess at the hem edge and rehem.

Place the gathered edge of the frill against the skirt, having right side of frill facing you, so that hem edge of frill just touches the ground. Mark the position of frill on skirt with a pin, then sew frill to skirt through the gathers.

To finish the bodice

Sew fastenings to back edges of bodice and skirt opening.

For the shoulder pieces, cut two 22 x 70cm (8½ x 28in) strips of fabric. Join the long edges of each strip, turn right side out and press. Sew lace edging to one long edge of each strip.

Pleat up one short end of each strip tightly and oversew, to hold in place and to neaten the raw edges. Put the dress on the child and pin these pleated short ends to centre front of the skirt, about 4cm (1½in) below the waist seam. Pin the shoulder pieces over the shoulder straps to cover them, then take them to the waist edge of bodice at the back. Trim off excess length of shoulder pieces, just below the level of bodice waist seam at the back. Turn in and gather these ends and pin level with the waist seam.

The piece of white lace fabric now has to be positioned on the front of the bodice, before you sew the shoulder pieces in place. Hem one edge of the lace fabric and stitch on a strip of lace edging. Having the dress on the child, place the lace piece inside the V-shape formed by the shoulder pieces, having the hemmed edge of lace about 5cm (2in) above the upper edge of the bodice. Trim off the other edges of lace to suit. Remove the dress and the shoulder pieces. Stitch lace piece to the bodice. Now sew the shoulder pieces to bodice and the shoulder straps as previously pinned.

Sew ribbon bow to the front of the dress as shown in the illustration.

UNDERSKIRT
You will need
3.70m (4yd) of plain cotton fabric (or you can use an old bed-sheet if available)
Fastening for waistband

To make
Cut and make up the skirt pieces as for the dress skirt. Gather the waist edge to fit the child's waist.

For the waistband, cut a 10cm (4in) wide strip of fabric, the child's waist measurement, plus 5cm (2in) for the end seams and an overlap. Use this strip to bind the gathered waist edge of the skirt. Sew fastener to ends of waistband.

Cut and make the hem frill as for the dress. Attach to the skirt as for the dress, having the hem edge of the frill just above ground level.

HAIR ORNAMENTS AND FAN
You will need
A few artificial flowers
Lengths of narrow ribbon
Two hair-grips
A fan from a toyshop

To make
Arrange the flowers in two groups, twisting the stems together. Bend around the stems to form loops which can be fixed around the hairgrips. Sew small loops of ribbon to the flower stems to hang below the flowers as shown in the illustration.

Pirate

For this outfit, a pair of ordinary pants can be adjusted temporarily to make the knee-breeches. Instructions are given for making the pirate hat, but you could buy one from a toyshop if the costume is required at short notice.

BASIS FOR COSTUME
A striped, short-sleeved T-shirt
Striped socks
A large handkerchief or scarf for neckerchief
A belt
A sword and sheath from a toyshop
A pair of black slip-on gym-shoes
Ordinary pants

KNEE BREECHES
If the pants are cast-offs, they can be altered permanently by cutting off the legs below knee-length, hemming the raw edges and threading elastic through to fit the child's legs.

To alter the pants temporarily, make bands of elastic to fit the child's legs below the knee. Put elastic bands on the child's legs. Turn up the legs of the pants to the inside, tucking them inside the elastic bands.

BUCKLED SHOES
You will need
Small pieces of black felt
Two silver buckles with centre shanks
    measuring about 3cm (1¼in)
Adhesive

To make
Trace the buckle-flap pattern off the page by the solid outline as shown, then cut out. Trim the pattern to shape at dotted lines shown, adjusting width so that narrow end of pattern will slot through your buckles.

Cut four buckle flaps from felt and glue them together in pairs. If the buckles have centre prongs, remove them. Sew the centre shanks of buckles to fronts of the gym-shoes, having the centre shanks horizontal. Thread the flaps through buckles and glue the narrow end of each flap to the inside of the buckle.

HAT
You will need
40cm (½yd) of 91cm (36in) wide black felt
80cm (⅞yd) of 82cm (32¼in) wide firm
    iron-on interfacing
1.30m (1½yd) of red bias binding
Scraps of white felt and a black marker pen for
    skull and cross-bones motif
Black stretchy fabric, such as could be cut off
    the leg of thick nylon tights or stocking
Adhesive

To make
Make a paper pattern for the hat brim by drawing a 38cm (15in) diameter circle with a 16cm (6½in) diameter circle at the centre. Cut out the centre circle. This will fit a head size of about 50cm (20in). Try the paper pattern on the child's head and enlarge centre hole if necessary.

Cut two hat-brim pieces from the interfacing and iron each one onto the felt. Cut out two more brims from interfacing and iron them

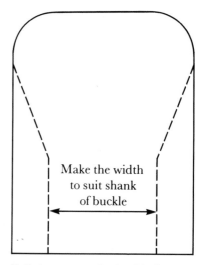

Make the width
to suit shank
of buckle

Full size pattern for buckle flap

on top of the first interfacing pieces in order to give extra firmness. Cut out the two felt brims level with the edges of the interfacing.

Now spread adhesive on one interfacing side of one brim at outer and inner edges. Place it on the other brim piece, interfacing sides together. Stitch round close to the inner and outer edges of the brim. Bind the outer edge with bias binding.

Cut a skull and cross-bones motif as shown in the illustration, then glue to the brim. Mark face on the skull with pen.

For the crown of the hat, cut a 15cm (6in) wide strip of stretchy fabric, long enough to go round the inner edge of hat brim when slightly stretched. Join the 15cm (6in) edges of the strip. Turn in one long edge a fraction and pin it to inner edge of brim, stretching to fit. Oversew the edge in place.

Gather up the remaining long edge of the strip, pull tight and fasten off, making sure that this gathered raw edge will be on the *inside* of

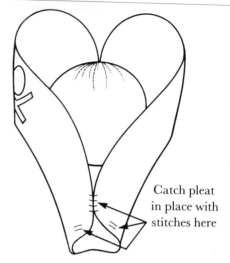

Catch pleat in place with stitches here

DIAGRAM *sewing the pleats in the hat*

the hat when worn.

Make a pleat at each side of the hat and catch it in place with stitches as shown in the diagram.

Crusader

If the required ordinary garments are available, this is one of the quickest costumes to put together. Instructions are given for the waist and sword belt, but you may have suitable belts on hand also. If possible, the garments should be all the same colour, either dark blue, grey or black.

BASIS FOR COSTUME
Long-sleeved sweater
Tights
Balaclava hood
A sword and sheath of the type illustrated, from a toyshop

BELTS
You will need
Two small buckles
Lengths of leather cloth to suit widths of buckles

To make
One belt should be long enough to go round the child's waist on top of the tunic and sweater. The sword belt should be much longer, to hang down the side as shown in the illustration. Attach one end of each belt strip to a buckle and make holes in the other ends.

TUNIC
You will need
70cm (¾yd) of 91cm (36in) wide white cotton fabric*
10cm (⅛yd) of 91cm (36in) wide red felt
1.70m (1⅞yd) of white bias binding
A 16cm (6in) length of Velcro
Metric or imperial graph paper

*Note: The amount of fabric quoted will make

a finished tunic length of about 62cm (25in) from shoulder to hem edge. The tunic should be just above knee length on the child. After making the pattern, try it against the child and adjust lower edge to correct length. If lower edge needs to be lengthened, add this amount to fabric requirements.

When fastened under the arms, the tunic measures about 66cm (26in) around the chest. If a larger chest measurement is required, add one quarter the extra amount to each side edge of the tunic pattern. Remember that the chest size of the tunic should be large enough to fit comfortably over the sweater. Adding extra to the side edges of the pattern will make no difference to fabric requirements.

To make

Copy the pattern outline onto graph paper square by square. Fold the white fabric, bringing the selvedges together. Pin the tunic pattern to double fabric and cut out.

For the cross, cut one 5 x 35cm (2 x 14in) strip of red felt and one 5 x 18cm (2 x 7in) strip. Sew them to one of the tunic pieces as shown on the pattern.

Join tunic pieces at the shoulder edges. Bind the neck edge and the armhole edges with bias binding. Narrowly hem the side and lower edges of the tunic.

Cut the furry and hooked Velcro strips into four equal lengths. Sew them to the sides of the tunic from armholes downwards as shown in the diagram.

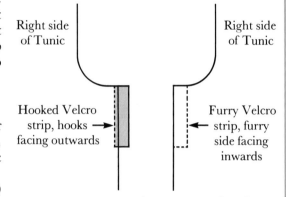

DIAGRAM *sewing Velcro strips to sides of tunic*

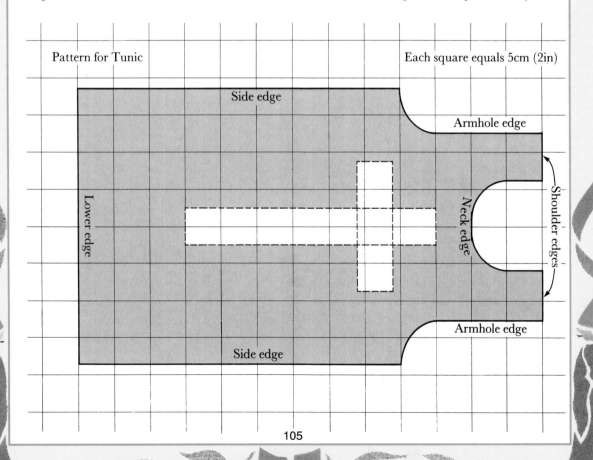

Viking

The helmet, spearhead and shoes are all made from felt.

BASIS FOR COSTUME
Ordinary pants or tracksuit pants
Ordinary shoes
A baggy long or short-sleeved T-shirt,
   reaching to the upper thighs
A belt

PANTS
The pants look best if they are elasticated at
the lower edges. If ordinary pants are used, unpick a little of the hem seam and thread elastic
through to fit the child's ankles.

TUNIC
Buy enough fancy braid to go around the lower
edge of the T-shirt. Stitch in place. Fasten belt
around the waist of tunic when worn.

FELT SHOES
You will need
Brown felt (see below)*
A pair of extra long football or sports-shoe laces

*Note: Before buying the felt, make a paper
pattern as follows. Take the child's ordinary
shoe and measure from the top of the shoe at
the heel end, under the sole and up over the
front of the shoe. Note the measurement.

   Next, measure the shoe from one side at the
top edge, under the sole to the other side at the
top edge. Note the measurement. Cut a rect-
angular paper pattern from the measurements,
then round off all the corners to make an oval
shape. You need enough felt to cut two pieces
using this oval pattern.

To make
Cut two oval shapes from felt. Snip small holes
at about 2.5cm (1in) intervals all round each
felt piece 1cm (3/8in) away from the edges.
Make sure you have an *even* number of holes.

Thread the laces through the holes, having
the long ends of the laces coming out at narrow
ends of the ovals.

   Put the ordinary shoes on the child. Place
feet at centre of the felt shoes and pull up the
laces tightly at centre front and knot. Wind
laces around the ankles, then up the pants legs
to the knees, crossing over laces as shown in
the illustration. Knot ends of laces.

CLOAK

You will need
A 75cm (30in) square of plain fabric
A large fancy brooch

Note: Non-woven curtain fabric is used for the cloak illustrated, but a square of shaggy fur fabric could be used instead.

To make
Hem all the raw edges. Fasten two corners of the cloak with the brooch at the front.

SPEAR

You will need
A 100cm (39in) length of 1cm (³⁄₈in) diameter wooden dowelling
A 20 x 30cm (10 x 12in) piece of dark-grey felt
Short lengths of braid
Stuffing or cotton-wool
Adhesive

To make
Trace the spearhead pattern off the page onto folded paper, placing fold in paper to edge indicated. Cut out, then open up paper to give full-size pattern. Cut two pieces from felt. Join them around the edges, taking a tiny seam and leaving lower edges open. Insert stuffing, pushing it in with the end of a pencil or similar and leaving the narrow lower portion unstuffed.

Spread glue on one end of the dowelling. Push it inside the straight portion of the spearhead. Glue braid around the narrow portion of the spearhead at lower edge and upper part of the narrow portion.

HELMET

You will need
20cm (¼yd) of 91cm (36in) wide dark-grey felt
20cm (¼yd) of 91cm (36in) wide black felt
20cm (¼yd) of 82cm (32¼in) wide firm iron-on interfacing
1.50m (1¾yd) of narrow black braid
Oddment of thin card
Adhesive

Note: Trace the helmet pattern off the page onto folded paper, placing fold in paper to edge indicated. Cut out, then open up paper to give full-size pattern. The helmet is made up of four of these pieces, oversewn together at the side edges. When made up from the pattern as traced, the lower edge of the helmet measures about 60cm (23¾in) around. Measure around the child's head from forehead to back, to see if this size will suit. It is better to make the helmet larger than necessary because the size can be adjusted later on. If the child's head measurement is larger than 60cm (23¾in), then add *one eighth* of the extra amount to each side edge of the pattern. Even a very small amount added to the pattern will make a big difference, so measure carefully.

To make
Cut eight helmet pieces from interfacing. Iron four of these separately onto the grey felt. Iron the remaining four pieces on top of the first interfacing pieces in order to give extra firmness.

Cut out the felt pieces level with the edges of the interfacing pieces. Oversew one pair of pieces together at one side edge for about 2cm (¾in), starting at lower edge. Oversew the remaining pair in the same way. Join the pairs at the remaining side edges, oversewing for 2cm (¾in) only as before. Now try the helmet on the child to see if the lower edge fits. If it is too large, unpick oversewing stitches and trim a little off side edges of pieces as required.

Now join the pieces by oversewing side edges together as before, but continue oversewing to the top points. Turn helmet right side out.

Glue on strips of braid over the seams, from lower edge across top point to other lower edge. Glue braid around the lower edge of helmet also.

Trace wing pattern off the page onto paper and cut out. Cut four wings from black felt. Cut two pieces of card to the shape shown by the dotted line on the wing pattern. Glue the wings together in pairs, sandwiching the card pieces between them.

Place the wings at sides of helmet so that the braid on the helmet is in the position shown on the wing pattern. Sew wings to helmet at lower and front edges of wings, between the dots as shown on the pattern.

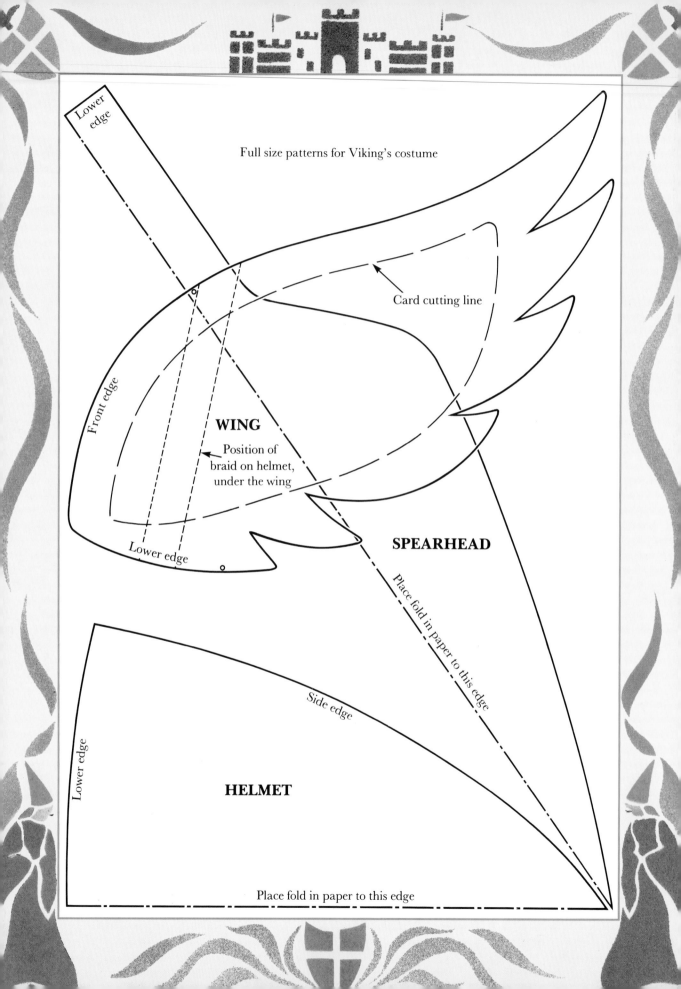

Full size patterns for Viking's costume

Lower edge

Card cutting line

Front edge

WING

Position of braid on helmet, under the wing

Lower edge

SPEARHEAD

Place fold in paper to this edge

Side edge

Lower edge

HELMET

Place fold in paper to this edge

Gypsy Dancer

A sleeveless T-shirt is used for the bodice of this costume, with strips of yellow fabric sewn to the armholes and neck edges, to form the blouse. If the child has a suitable blouse, the T-shirt can be worn over it instead. An inexpensive plastic tambourine from a toyshop can be prettied up with braid, ribbons, and a paper rose motif.

BASIS FOR COSTUME
A sleeveless T-shirt
A pair of flip-flop sandals or tap-dancing shoes
A large square chiffon scarf and a few large sequins
A pair of clip-on gold hooped earrings
A plastic tambourine from a toyshop

SKIRT AND HEADSCARF
You will need
1.70m (1⅞yd) of 91cm (36in) wide printed cotton fabric*
2m (2¼yd) of 91cm (36in) wide soft white net fabric, such as curtain net*
3.30m (3⅝yd) of jumbo ric-rac braid
Fastenings for waistband and skirt opening

*Note: The amounts of fabric quoted will make a skirt length of 52cm (21in) from waist to lower edge of the *white net* frill. The skirt is composed of three frills of printed fabric, of different widths. To shorten it, any excess can be trimmed off the top frill before gathering the waist edge.

To lengthen the skirt, the lowest frill can be made deeper, but you will need to add three times the extra skirt length needed, to the printed fabric requirements, and six times the extra length to the net fabric requirements.

To make the frills
First cut an 8cm (3in) wide strip off one end of the printed fabric, across the full 91cm (36in) width. Lay this aside for the waistband.

For the top skirt frill, cut a 14cm (5½in) wide strip across the full 91cm (36in) width of the printed fabric.

For the middle frill, cut two 18cm (7in) wide strips across the full width of the printed fabric. Join the strips at one pair of short edges.

Gather one long edge to fit one 91cm (36in) edge of the top frill strip. Stitch in place, having right sides together and raw edges level.

For the lower frill, cut three 22cm (9in) wide strips (or required width if you are lengthening the skirt), across the full width of the printed fabric. Join the strips at the short edges to make one length. Gather one long edge to fit the long raw edge of the middle frill and stitch in place as before. Hem the remaining long raw edge of this frill and stitch ric-rac to right side of the hem.

To make up the skirt
Join the short edges of all the frills for centre-back seam of skirt, taking a 2cm (¾in) seam and leaving 18cm (7in) open at top of seam for back skirt opening. Press seam to one side and neaten raw edges of the opening.

Gather the waist edge of the skirt to child's waist measurement, allowing a little extra for an overlap. Use the waistband strip to bind gathered edge of skirt, trimming the strip of fabric to length required. Sew fasteners to ends of waistband and skirt opening.

The net hem frill
Put the skirt on the child and measure from gathéred top of the lowest frill to ground level. Double this measurement and cut three strips this width, across the full 91cm (36in) width of the net fabric. Join the strips to each other at the short edges to form a continuous length. Fold the strip, having the right side outside and bringing the long raw edges together. Gather along the folded edge and pull up gathers to fit the gathered edge of the lowest frill. Sew gathered edge of net to lowest frill seam on the inside of the skirt.

From the remaining net fabric, cut five 8cm

(3in) wide strips across the full width of the fabric. Join ends to form a continuous length. Gather at one long edge to fit around the outer layer of the net frill, then sew in place, having lower edges of both frills level.

To make the headscarf

From the remaining piece of cotton fabric, cut a 25cm (10in) wide strip across the full width of the fabric. Stitch ric-rac braid to the right side of the fabric at the short ends, 3cm (1¼in) away from the raw edges. Fold strip with right side inside, bringing the long edges together. Join raw edges, leaving a gap for turning. Trim seam and corners, turn right side out and press. Slip stitch gap.

BODICE AND BLOUSE

You will need
A long coloured football-boot lace or
    sports-shoe lace
50cm (½yd) of 91cm (36in) wide non-fray
    thin polyester jersey fabric
70cm (¾yd) of narrow elastic

To make

Place the T-shirt on a flat surface with the front uppermost. Place a piece of card, or a magazine inside it, between the front and back. Mark a line up the centre front with pins. Now pin the shoe-lace up the front, zig-zag fashion as far as the neck edge as shown in the illustration, having the long ends of the shoe-lace at the neck edge. Sew in place as pinned, then tie ends of shoe-lace in a bow at neck edge.

For neck portion of the blouse, cut an 8 x 75cm (3 x 30in) strip across the 91cm (36in)

width of the fabric. Join short ends of the strip. Turn one long edge 1cm (⅜in) to wrong side and stitch down raw edge, leaving a gap for threading through the elastic.

Gather the remaining long raw edge to fit inside the neck edge of the T-shirt. Pin the edge in place, then catch to inside of T-shirt with loose oversewing stitches, so that the stitches will give when the garment is put on.

Thread elastic through the casing. Put the garment on the child and pull up the elastic to gather fabric as necessary to fit neatly. Join ends of elastic and close gap in stitching.

For each sleeve, cut a 16 x 60cm (6¼ x 24in) strip, across the 91cm (36in) width of the fabric. Trim one long edge of each sleeve to a curved shape as shown in the diagram below.

Join the underarm edges of each sleeve. Turn in and stitch the long straight edges to form casings for the elastic, in same way as for the neck piece. Thread elastic through to fit child's upper arms. Join ends of elastic and close gaps in stitching.

Gather along top raw edges of sleeves to fit inside the armholes of T-shirt and sew in place as for the neck piece.

SASH

Use the chiffon scarf, folding it corner to corner and rolling up at centre before tying around the waist. Sew sequins to the corners of scarf which will hang down after tying.

TAMBOURINE

Glue a circle of card to the top of the tambourine and a flower motif cut from a magazine to the centre. Stick braid around the card circle as shown in the illustration. Add lengths of ribbon.

DIAGRAM *trimming the fabric strip for sleeve*

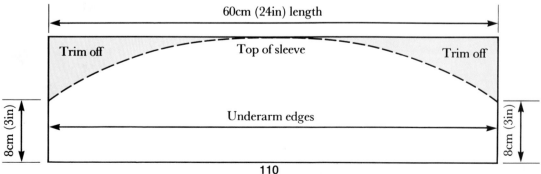

Supergirl

Everyday items of clothing, such as tights and a long-sleeved T-shirt, are used as a basis for this costume. The other items – tabard, cuffs and headband – can be made very quickly from quilted fabric, trimmed with glittery braid.

BASIS FOR COSTUME

Tights
Leotard or bathing suit or coloured knickers
Long-sleeved T-shirt or sweater
A space-gun from a toyshop
A pair of slipperettes or suitable shoes

TABARD, CUFFS AND HEADBAND

You will need
70cm (¾yd) of 152cm (60in) wide quilted fabric
3m (3⅜yd) of 1cm (⅜in) wide sequin and lurex braid
2 hooks and eyes
3 buttons, 5cm (2in) diameter
3 buttons, 1.5cm (½in) diameter
Scrap of contrasting coloured fabric and fancy braid for the 'S' motif
Short length of narrow elastic
Bit of sparkly junk jewellery or a buckle, for headband decoration
A 25cm (10in) length of Velcro
Metric or imperial graph paper

Note: The tabard measures 44cm (17½in) from shoulder to lower edge when finished, and 58cm (23in) around the waist when fastened at the sides. It can be widened at the sides and lengthened at the lower edge as required, making no difference to the fabric requirements, as can be seen from the cutting layout.

To make the tabard

Copy the pattern outline onto graph paper square by square.

Referring to the cutting layout, cut two tabard pieces, folding the fabric for each one and placing edge of pattern indicated to fold each time.

Cut one of the pieces open along the fold line. Rejoin these edges, leaving 9cm (3½in) open at neck edge of the seam for the centre-back opening. Turn in and stitch down seam allowance on the open edges.

Join the front tabard to back at the shoulder edges. Turn in all the outer raw edges 1cm (⅜in) and stitch down. Do not turn in the neck edge, but clip curves within seam allowance.

For the collar, cut a 10 x 54cm (4 x 21¼in) strip of fabric. Tack, then stitch, one long edge of collar strip to neck edge of tabard, right sides together, raw edges level, and letting the short ends of collar strip extend 1cm (⅜in) beyond edges of the back neck opening. Fold remaining long raw edge of collar to inside and oversew it to the collar seam. Turn in and slip stitch short ends of collar. Sew the hooks and eyes to ends of collar. Sew braid around the collar close to the seam.

Place the tabard on the child and mark position of waist with pins at the side edges of tabard pieces. Cut two 5cm (2in) lengths of furry and of hooked Velcro strip. Sew the hooked strips in position on back tabard piece at sides, as shown in Diagram 1, with hooks facing outwards. Sew the corresponding furry

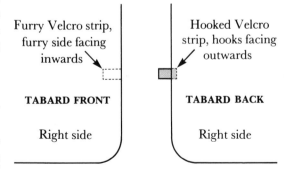

Furry Velcro strip, furry side facing inwards →

Hooked Velcro strip, hooks facing outwards ←

TABARD FRONT

Right side

TABARD BACK

Right side

DIAGRAM 1 *sewing Velcro strips to waist position on tabard*

strips in place on wrong side of front tabard with furry sides facing inwards.

For the 'S' motif, cut an 8cm (3in) square from the contrast colour fabric. Sew on the braid, forming it into an 'S' shape as shown in the illustration. Now either machine satin stitch the motif in place just below the collar, or turn in the raw edges of fabric a little and stitch in place.

To make the belt

Referring to the cutting layout, cut a 10cm (4in) wide strip of fabric by the measurement around the child's waist over the tabard, adding 2cm (¾in) to this measurement.

Turn in all the raw edges 1cm (⅜in) and stitch down. Sew on lengths of braid near to the long edges of the belt. Sew Velcro strips to ends of the belt as shown in Diagram 2, trimming the lengths of Velcro to fit.

Add the buttons to the front of the belt, sewing the smaller buttons to the larger buttons.

To make the headband

Cut an 8 x 50cm (3 x 20in) strip of fabric. Turn in raw edges and stitch down as for belt. Sew a length of braid down the centre of the strip and add the oddment of jewellery to centre front. Sew a short length of elastic to the ends so that headband fits the child's head comfortably.

To make the cuffs

Copy the pattern outline from the diagram onto graph paper. Cut two cuff pieces, placing the pattern to fold each time as shown on the cutting layout. Join the side edges of each cuff, leaving 7cm (2¾in) open at wrist ends of seams. Turn in seam allowance on these openings and stitch down. Turn in and stitch down wrist and upper edges also, clipping at curves. Sew braid near to upper edges of cuffs. Sew 2.5cm (1in) Velcro strips near to wrist edges of cuffs in same way as for the tabard.

CAPE

You will need
50cm (⅝yd) of 91cm (36in) wide shiny fabric
A 30cm (12in) length of narrow elastic
2 large snap-fasteners

To make

Narrowly hem the edges of the fabric, except for one 91cm (36in) edge. Turn in and hem this edge to form a casing for the elastic. Thread the elastic through and sew ends to each end of the casing.

Sew the halves of the snap-fasteners to the ends of the casing. Sew the remaining halves of the snap fasteners to the back of the tabard close to the collar so that the cape can be attached.

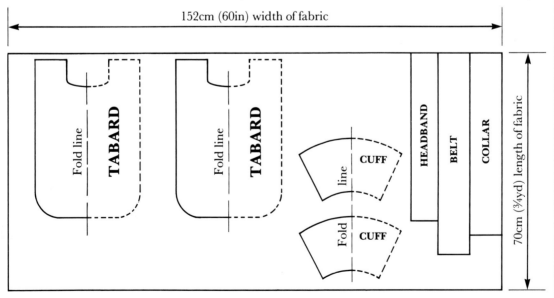
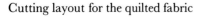

Cutting layout for the quilted fabric

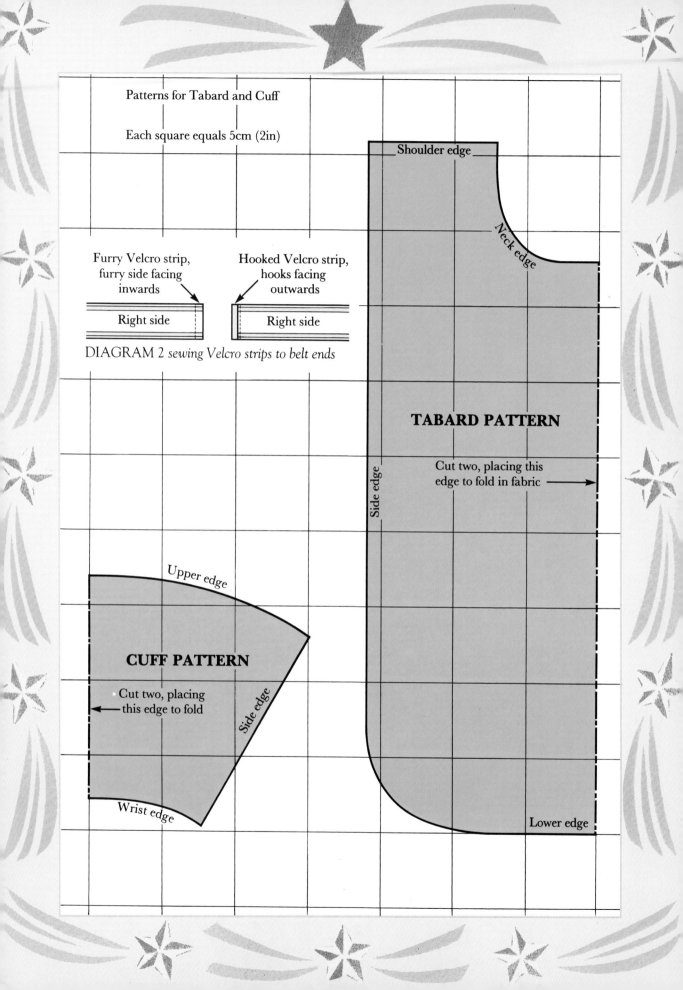

Patterns for Tabard and Cuff

Each square equals 5cm (2in)

Furry Velcro strip, furry side facing inwards

Hooked Velcro strip, hooks facing outwards

Right side

Right side

DIAGRAM 2 *sewing Velcro strips to belt ends*

Shoulder edge

Neck edge

TABARD PATTERN

Side edge

Cut two, placing this edge to fold in fabric →

Upper edge

CUFF PATTERN

• Cut two, placing ← this edge to fold

Side edge

Wrist edge

Lower edge

Superboy

The red and yellow short wellington boots set the colour scheme for this outfit, which also uses other items of everyday clothing. The additional items – belt, collar, cape and cuffs – are all quick to make.

BASIS FOR COSTUME
Short wellington boots
A long-sleeved T-shirt or sweater
Tights
Bathing-trunks
A space-gun from a toyshop

COLLAR, BELT AND CUFFS
You will need
30cm (⅜yd) of 152cm (60in) wide quilted
    fabric
1.40m (1⅝yd) of 1.5cm (⅝in) wide braid
A circular plastic lid (off a margarine tub or
    similar carton)
4 matching fancy buttons with shanks
One other fancy button with a shank
A 20cm (8in) length of Velcro
Adhesive

To make the collar
For the collar pattern, draw a 25cm (10in) square onto paper, then cut an 8cm (3in) diameter hole from the centre for the neck edge of the collar.

Referring to the cutting layout, cut two collar pieces from fabric. Cut each collar piece open from one corner of the square to the neck edge, as shown on the cutting layout. These cut edges will be the centre-back edges of the collar.

Join the collar pieces around the outer edges, the centre-back edges and neck edges, leaving a gap in one straight edge for turning. Trim the corners and clip curve in neck seam. Turn collar right side out and press, then slip stitch gap.

Sew braid all around the outer square edge of the collar, within the seamed edges. Cut a 4cm (1½in) strip of hooked and of furry Velcro. Sew the strips to back opening of the collar, near to neck edge as shown in Diagram 1.

Place the collar on the child on top of the T-shirt and fasten Velcro at back. Mark position of the lower point at front, on the T-shirt. Remove garments. Cut a 2cm (¾in) length of hooked and of furry Velcro. Sew one strip to lower front point of the collar on the wrong side and the other strip to front of T-shirt above the pin.

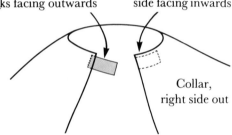

Hooked Velcro strip, hooks facing outwards

Furry Velcro strip, furry side facing inwards

Collar, right side out

DIAGRAM 1 *sewing Velcro strips to collar*

To make the belt
Referring to cutting layout, cut a 14cm (5½in) wide strip of fabric by the child's waist measurement, plus 2cm (¾in). Bring the long edges of the belt strip together and join the raw edges, leaving a gap for turning. Trim corners, turn right side out and press, then slip stitch gap. Cut a strip of hooked and of furry Velcro to fit short ends of the belt. Stitch strips in place as shown in Diagram 2.

Furry Velcro strip, furry side facing inwards

Hooked Velcro strip, hooks facing outwards

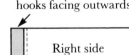

Right side

Right side

DIAGRAM 2 *sewing Velcro strips to belt ends*

If the plastic lid has lettering on it, either remove this by rubbing with a scouring pad or glue on a circle of paper.

Pierce a hole at the centre of the plastic lid, then glue on the single button, pushing the shank through the hole. Glue on the other four buttons in the same way, spacing them equally around the first button as shown in the illustration. To secure the buttons, pass a double strand of sewing thread through each of the holes in the shanks to link all the buttons together, then knot the ends of the thread.

Sew the centre button to the centre front of the belt. Sew the buttons on either side to the belt also.

To make the cuffs
Referring to the cutting layout, cut four 10 x 18cm (4 x 7in) strips of fabric. Join the pieces in pairs, leaving a gap in each seam for turning. Trim seams and corners, then turn right side out. Press cuffs, then slip stitch gaps. Sew braid to one long edge of each cuff in the same way as

for the collar. These braid-trimmed edges will be the top edges of cuffs, the opposite long edges fasten around the wrists with Velcro. Sew Velcro strips to the cuffs in exactly the same way as for the collar.

CAPE
You will need
50cm (⅝yd) of 91cm (36in) wide fabric
30cm (⅜yd) of bias binding to match the fabric
2 large snap-fasteners

To make
Narrowly hem the edges except for one 91cm (36in) edge. Gather this edge to measure 25cm (10in). Bind it with bias binding. Sew snap-fastener halves to each end of the binding. Sew corresponding halves of fasteners to shoulders of T-shirt near to neck edge so that cape can be attached.

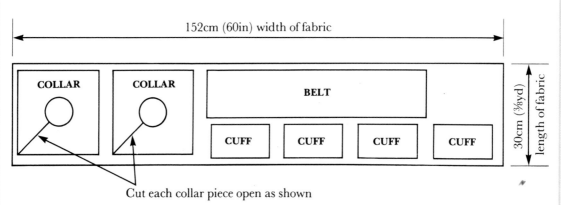

Cut each collar piece open as shown

Cutting layout for quilted fabric pieces

English/American Glossary

English	American
DRAWING-PIN	Thumb tack
FUR FABRIC	Fake fur
NYLON TIGHTS	Nylon pantyhose
RIC-RAC	Rickrack
SHIRRING ELASTIC	Elastic thread
SNAP-FASTENERS	Snaps
UHU GLUE	Tacky glue or Slomons

Acknowledgements

The costumes in this book were originally featured in *Woman's Weekly* magazine and the author would like to express her thanks to the Editor and all Home Department staff for their assistance and co-operation during the preparation of all the material included. The author and publishers also wish to thank IPC magazines, publishers of *Woman's Weekly,* for their kind permission to reproduce their photographs.

Index